The easyCOOK
COOKBOOK

10 9 8 7 6 5 4 3 2 1

Published in 2009 by BBC Books, an imprint of Ebury Publishing.
A Random House Group Company

Recipes © BBC Magazines 2009
Photographs © BBC Magazines 2009
Book design © Woodlands Books 2009
With thanks to BBC *Good Food* magazine, where these recipes have previously
appeared.

The Random House Group Limited Reg. No. 954009

Addresses for companies within the Random House Group can be found at
www.randomhouse.co.uk

A CIP catalogue record for this book is available from the British Library.

ISBN 9781846077470

The Random House Group Limited supports The Forest Stewardship Council
(FSC), the leading international forest certification organisation. All our titles that
are printed on Greenpeace approved FSC certified paper carry the FSC logo. Our
paper procurement policy can be found at www.rbooks.co.uk/environment

Commissioning editor: Muna Reyal
Project editor: Laura Higginson
Designer: Kathryn Gammon
Picture researcher: Gabby Harrington
Editorial assistance: Marie-Louise Stevens
Production: David Brimble

Colour origination, printing and binding by Butler Tanner & Dennis Ltd

Mixed Sources
Product group from well-managed
forests and other controlled sources
www.fsc.org Cert no. SGS-COC-005091
© 1996 Forest Stewardship Council

FSC

The easy COOK
COOKBOOK
REAL FOOD FOR BUSY PEOPLE

Edited by Sarah Giles

BBC
BOOKS

Contents

Introduction

Easy Cook magazine does exactly what its title suggests – it makes cooking easy! And this cookbook is designed to show you just how straightforward making home-cooked meals can be.

It's easy to get stuck in a rut, making the same meals week in and week out – and it's no wonder that cooking can sometimes seem like a chore. But *Easy Cook* shows you new ways of using familiar ingredients, with plenty of recipes you can rustle up and get on the table in a matter of minutes – safe in the knowledge that you're serving yourself and your family healthy, home-cooked food. These are not the sort of recipes you have to spend hours on – they're fast, simple ideas that need no special skills and, more often than not, they use the kind of ingredients you would normally put in your supermarket trolley every week anyway.

There's now at least one whole generation in the UK that has not been taught cookery at school and, without the basic skills, cooking from scratch can seem daunting. What's more, with so much convenience food around it's tempting to think – why bother? However, a growing number of us are coming to realize that while convenience food does have a place in our busy lives, too much of it is simply not good for us. And, as you'll see from the recipes in this, our first *Easy Cook*

cookbook, it can be almost as quick and easy to make a meal yourself as it is to heat up a ready meal.

Quick and easy cooking

That's not to say we insist our readers turn their backs on anything that's been pre-prepared. Cooking doesn't have to be all or nothing and our recipes often include short-cut ingredients – after all, *Easy Cook*'s strapline is 'real food for busy people' and we know that time is of the essence. So we're quite happy to suggest using a sachet of ready-made stir-fry sauce or a tub of pasta sauce in an ingredients list, for example – there's nothing wrong with that when the recipe includes nutritious, fresh ingredients too. As well as short-cut ingredients, the recipes are full of time-saving techniques that you can use again and again and, to give you as much choice and flexibility as possible, we also suggest lots of variations – showing you how to adapt a recipe so it's suitable for vegetarians, for example, or explaining how, with an adjustment or two, you can change a chicken recipe to a fish recipe or use lamb instead of beef.

When we put together the first issues of *Easy Cook* magazine, over four years ago, our aim was to encourage beginners to get cooking. But it soon became obvious that our no-fuss recipes were appealing to more experienced cooks too. After all, even if you're the best cook in the world, there are still times when you need inspiration for a quick meal at the end of a busy day! We like to think our straightforward approach, friendly tone and wide selection of ideas, ranging from after-work suppers to cakes, bakes and meals for entertaining, continue to give everyone – keen cook or not-so-keen – plenty of new recipes to add to their repertoire.

Meals for the whole week

Following the same distinctive format as the magazine, *The Easy Cook Cookbook* is divided into two parts. The first part, 'Easy Everyday Food', starts with our trademark 'Easy Suppers' (all ready in 20 minutes or less) and you'll find plenty more ideas for family dinners in the 'Easy Family Food' chapter, which is designed to help get the whole family back round the dining table once in a while – after all, there's plenty of evidence to suggest that families who eat together find it easier to communicate with each other. Our 'Easy Standby' recipes take some of our favourite storecupboard ingredients as their starting point, while 'Easy Puds' gives you speedy ideas for rounding off weeknight meals. And with our 'Easy Low-fat Meals', you'll find that cutting down on fat doesn't mean missing out on flavour.

The second part of the cookbook is called 'Easy Weekend Food' and this is where, if you need any more convincing, you'll really see how enjoyable time spent in the kitchen can be. The recipes are all still straightforward and none of them requires you to spend ages standing over the stove, but they're designed for more relaxed cooking and dining than most of us have time for during the week. So you'll find a pie, a casserole and a roast, for example, that take a little more time in the oven than recipes in 'Easy Everyday Food' – but you can just leave them cooking while you get on with enjoying your weekend. You'll find recipes for cakes and bakes that will remind you how therapeutic cooking can be – especially when you can sit back with a cuppa afterwards and reward yourself with a slice of something delicious. And there are also lots of recipes in this part of the cookbook that are perfect for entertaining – you can mix and match our suggested starters, main courses and desserts, but feel free to substitute recipes from other parts of the book too.

We really hope *The Easy Cook Cookbook* will inspire you – whether you're an experienced cook or a beginner – and that it will motivate you to get into the kitchen and do some more home cooking. Remember – it's fun, it's easy (and it's tasty, cheaper and healthier too).

Happy cooking!

Sarah Giles

PART ONE

easy everyday food

Great recipes for midweek meals, to take you through from Monday to Friday

Most of us are busy, busy, busy these days, especially during the working week. If you come home tired after a day at the office, or you've been coping with the kids all day, it's so easy to turn to a ready meal for supper – and, every day, thousands of people do just that.

The recipes in our 'Easy Everyday Food' section are designed to show you that good, home-cooked food using fresh, healthy ingredients doesn't need to take ages to prepare and that ready meals and fast food really aren't the only options when life is hectic and time is short.

Whether you're a busy mum, or you go out to work all day, you'll find plenty of easy evening meals that can be on the table in 20 minutes or less. There are also recipes that can be rustled up using the kind of ingredients most of us already have in our kitchen cupboards, meals that even the fussiest of kids will love, speedy puddings and – if you're on a diet – you'll find lots of low-fat options too.

easy
SUPPERS
ready in 20 minutes or less

These suppers are designed to help you get good, nutritious food on the table at the end of a busy day and they can all be ready in no more than 20 minutes.

So many people rely on ready meals these days and, although we know they can come in handy sometimes, our aim is to show that in not much more than the time it takes to peel off the lid and cook one in the microwave, you can just as easily rustle up a simple homemade meal. It only takes a little more effort, but the end result is tastier and a lot less expensive.

Our easy suppers use everyday ingredients and give them a new twist. We try to keep the number of ingredients to a minimum too, so you don't have to spend ages looking through your kitchen cupboards before you can get started (and this helps keep the costs of each meal down too).

The method in each recipe usually involves just two or three different steps, and you don't need any special knowledge or skills to get good results. It means that all of the recipes are great if you're a beginner but, equally, if you're a more experienced cook you'll find plenty of ideas to inspire you.

Soy salmon

You can leave out the garlic in step 3, if you like, but it gives the salmon a really lovely flavour and is so quick and easy to do that it's worth spending just a couple of extra minutes on it.

- Serves 4
- Ready in 10 minutes
- Not suitable for freezing

4 salmon fillets
2 tbsp olive oil
4 tsp soy sauce
2 cloves of garlic, thinly sliced
3 spring onions, finely shredded

1 Turn on the grill to medium. Brush the salmon with a little oil and sprinkle with salt and pepper. Line a grill pan with foil, brush with a little more olive oil and put the salmon fillets on it, skin-side down. Sprinkle 1 tsp of soy sauce over each salmon fillet.

2 Grill the salmon on one side only for about 6–8 minutes, until the flesh is lightly browned and firm to the touch.

3 Fry the garlic in the remaining oil, stirring all the time until it just starts to turn golden.

Serve with the garlic, the shredded spring onions and new potatoes or stir-fried veg

Sticky glazed pork

Couscous makes a good alternative to rice for midweek suppers, as it's so quick to prepare. You can add cucumber, peppers or even frozen peas to this dish to increase the veg count, if you like.

- Serves 4
- Ready in 20 minutes
- Not suitable for freezing

4 tsp English mustard
3 tbsp clear honey
splash of orange juice
4 pork loin steaks
300g couscous
1 bunch spring onions, thinly sliced
1 tbsp olive oil
450ml hot chicken stock
large handful of cherry tomatoes,
    quartered

1 Turn on the grill to medium. Mix together the mustard, honey and orange juice, then smear over the steaks. Grill the steaks for 4 minutes on each side or until cooked, brushing over any leftover glaze.

2 Meanwhile, tip the couscous and spring onions into a bowl. Spoon the oil into the stock, pour onto the couscous and stir. Cover tightly with cling film and leave for 5–6 minutes or until the liquid is absorbed. Fluff up with a fork, then stir in the tomatoes and season. Top with the pork and pan juices.

Serve with green veg

Lamb steaks with tomatoes and olives

You could make this using chicken thighs or drumsticks instead of lamb, too. Don't use tinned black olives – they tend to be a bit hard and bullet-like. Buy fresh ones (from the deli counter in the supermarket) if you can or, failing that, use olives from a jar.

■ Serves 4
■ Ready in 20 minutes
■ Not suitable for freezing

2 tbsp olive oil
4 lamb leg steaks
1 red onion, cut into 8 wedges
2 tsp dried oregano
150ml white wine
400g pack cherry tomatoes
100g pitted black olives
handful of fresh flat-leaf parsley, chopped

1 Turn the oven to fan 180C/conventional 200C/gas 6. Heat the oil in a large roasting tin on the hob. Brown the lamb steaks in the tin for 1 minute each side.

2 Add the onion to the tin with the oregano. Pour over the wine and add the tomatoes. Scatter over the olives, then place the tin in the oven for 5 minutes until the lamb is cooked. Scatter with the parsley.

Sausages with mustard and apple

Use meaty sausages for this – herby ones like Lincolnshire will give the best flavour and stay nice and firm. To make this dish even speedier to cook, cut the sausages in half before you fry them.

- Serves 4
- Ready in 20 minutes
- Suitable for freezing

8 Lincolnshire sausages
1 tbsp olive oil
1 large onion, cut into thin wedges
2 apples, cored and cut into wedges
1 rounded tbsp redcurrant jelly
2 tbsp wholegrain mustard
1 chicken stock cube
a few fresh rosemary sprigs or ½ tsp dried (optional)

1 Fry the sausages in the oil for 5 minutes, turning frequently. Add the onion and cook until golden. Toss in the apples and stir-fry for a minute or so.

2 Pour 300ml of boiling water over the redcurrant jelly, mustard and stock cube, and stir well. Pour into the pan. Add the rosemary, if using, and simmer, uncovered, until the apples are just tender and the sausages are cooked through.

Serve with mash or rice

Honey mushroom chicken

The tasty sauce for this quick-cook chicken dish is lovely as it is but if you prefer a slightly thicker sauce, take the chicken from the pan at the end of step 2, turn up the heat and allow the liquid to bubble and reduce a little.

- Serves 4
- Ready in 20 minutes
- Suitable for freezing

4 boneless, skinless chicken breasts
2 tbsp olive oil
250g mushrooms, sliced
2 fresh rosemary sprigs, halved
2 tbsp tomato ketchup
1 tbsp clear honey
1 chicken stock cube

1 Cook the chicken in the oil for about 2 minutes each side. Remove from the pan then add the mushrooms and rosemary, and cook until starting to brown.

2 Stir in a mugful of water then add the ketchup and honey, and crumble in the stock cube. Put the chicken back in the pan. Cover and cook over a gentle heat for 10 minutes until just tender.

Serve with mashed potatoes and green veg

Tangy trout

Don't throw away leftover or stale bread – instead, whizz it into breadcrumbs and store it in the freezer, ready to use in a recipe like this (it will take no more than a couple of minutes to defrost).

- ■ Serves 4
- ■ Ready in 15 minutes
- ■ Not suitable for freezing

4 trout fillets, skin on
50g breadcrumbs
1 tbsp soft butter
small bunch of fresh parsley, chopped
grated rind and juice of 1 lemon
25g pine nuts, toasted and roughly chopped
1 tbsp olive oil

1 Turn on the grill to high. Lay the trout fillets, skin-side down, on an oiled baking tray. Mix together the breadcrumbs, butter, parsley, lemon rind and juice, and half the pine nuts. Scatter the mixture in a thin layer over the fillets, drizzle with the oil and place under the grill for 5 minutes. Sprinkle over the remaining pine nuts.

Serve with lemon wedges and a potato salad

Chicken with lemon and chives

Make a dressing for potato salad to serve with this dish, using equal quantities of mayonnaise and yogurt and a sprinkling of snipped chives, then reserve a little to spoon over each chicken breast too.

- ■ Serves 4
- ■ Ready in 10 minutes
- ■ Not suitable for freezing

4 boneless, skinless chicken breasts
2 tbsp olive oil
juice of ½ lemon
small handful of fresh chives, snipped

1 Put the chicken breasts between two sheets of cling film and bash with a rolling pin to flatten them out a little. Season with salt and pepper. Mix the olive oil, lemon juice and chives, then toss with the chicken.

2 Heat a griddle or large frying pan. Cook the chicken in batches for 6–8 minutes, turning halfway through.

Serve with a potato salad, lettuce and cherry tomatoes

Tuna linguine

You could use spaghetti or tagliatelle instead of linguine – any long, thin pasta will work well, so that the tuna sauce can cling to the individual strands. Recipes often suggest that you leave in chilli seeds if you like a hotter flavour, but it's best to take them out for this recipe as the extra heat would overpower the tuna.

■ Serves 4
■ Ready in 20 minutes
■ Not suitable for freezing

2 cloves of garlic, chopped
1 red chilli, deseeded and chopped
4 tbsp fresh parsley, chopped
4 tbsp olive oil
400g can chopped tomatoes
2 x 200g cans tuna in olive oil, drained
 and flaked
375g linguine

1 Fry the garlic and chilli with 3 tbsp of the parsley in the oil until soft. Add the tomatoes and cook for 3 minutes, then fold in the tuna, season and bubble for 10 minutes.

2 Meanwhile, cook the pasta according to pack instructions. Drain, then return to the pan. Pour in the tuna sauce and mix. Sprinkle over the remaining parsley.

Fusilli with green spinach sauce

If you're watching your weight, you could use low-fat cream cheese instead of the mascarpone, but be careful not to overheat the mixture or it may split. Don't be tempted to miss out the pine nuts, as they make a big difference to the overall taste and texture.

■ Serves 4
■ Ready in 15 minutes
■ Not suitable for freezing

400g fusilli
225g bag baby spinach
1 clove of garlic
250g tub mascarpone
juice of ½ large lemon
25g grated parmesan
50g pine nuts, lightly toasted

1 Cook the pasta according to pack instructions. Meanwhile, put half the spinach in a food processor with the garlic, mascarpone, lemon juice and parmesan, then whizz to a smooth sauce.

2 Drain the pasta thoroughly and return to the pan over a low heat. Stir in the sauce, pine nuts and remaining spinach, until the spinach has just wilted. Season well.

Serve with salad, and sprinkled with extra parmesan

Goat's cheese and leek tarts

As long as you don't use pastry that's already been frozen, these tarts can be frozen once assembled and kept for up to 2 months.

- Serves 4
- Ready in 20 minutes
- Suitable for freezing

1 tbsp olive oil
2 large leeks, sliced
2 rashers back bacon, chopped
one sheet ready-rolled puff pastry
1 tbsp crème fraîche
1 tbsp wholegrain or Dijon mustard
4 slices firm goat's cheese, from a 100g log

1 First cook the filling. Turn the oven to fan 200C/conventional 220C/gas 7. Heat the oil in a frying pan, then add the leeks and bacon. Cook for a further 5 minutes, season, then tip onto a plate to cool.

2 Unroll the pastry and cut out four 12x18cm rectangles. Lift them onto a baking sheet. Using the tip of a sharp knife, mark a border inside each one, about 1.5cm from the edge.

3 Mix the crème fraîche and mustard together, then spread over the inside of the pastry frames. Spoon the leek and bacon mix over the mustard mix, then place the goat's cheese on top. Bake for 15 minutes until the pastry is crisp and golden.

Serve with salad

Creamy chicken with leeks

We often use crème fraîche in *Easy Cook* recipes in place of cream – it's lighter and can give a better flavour, plus it's less likely to separate when it's heated.

- Serves 4
- Ready in 20 minutes
- Not suitable for freezing

6 rashers unsmoked, streaky bacon, chopped
1 tbsp olive oil
4 skinless, boneless chicken breasts, cut into strips
2 leeks, sliced
2 tbsp plain flour
600ml chicken stock
1 tbsp wholegrain mustard
3 tbsp crème fraîche

1 Fry the bacon in the oil for 2 minutes. Add the chicken, and cook for a further 3 minutes, until the pieces begin to turn golden. Tip in the leeks and cook gently for 10 minutes until wilted and tender.

2 Stir in the flour and gradually add the stock, stirring constantly. Add the mustard and crème fraîche, stir again then simmer gently for 5 minutes until the sauce is lightly thickened and creamy.

Serve with jacket potatoes

Lamb chops with a coriander crust

If you have any coriander topping left over, you can keep it in the fridge for a day or two – it's lovely stirred through pasta or served with grilled chicken.

- Serves 4
- Ready in 20 minutes
- Not suitable for freezing

3 tbsp olive oil
8 lamb loin chops
50g roasted peanuts
20g pack fresh coriander, roughly chopped
1 clove of garlic

1 Turn on the grill to medium. Rub a little oil on each side of the lamb, then season with salt and pepper. Grill for 5 minutes, then turn over and cook for 5 minutes more for medium, or 7 minutes for well done.

2 Meanwhile, whizz the remaining ingredients together with the rest of the oil in a blender to make a rough paste. Drizzle over the chops.

Serve with rice or couscous and green veg

Thai mince

Mince is perfect for quick family meals, but the finished dish can sometimes look a bit unexciting – adding fresh basil to this recipe at the last minute jazzes it up and adds a wonderful flavour too.

- Serves 4
- Ready in 20 minutes
- Suitable for freezing

1 onion, sliced
1 tbsp vegetable oil
1 clove of garlic, chopped
1 red pepper, deseeded and roughly chopped
500g pack turkey or pork mince
½ tsp chilli powder
2 tbsp soy sauce
175ml chicken stock
2 tsp cornflour
handful of fresh basil leaves

1 Fry the onion in the oil for 4 minutes until golden. Stir in the garlic and red pepper, and cook for 4 minutes, then add the mince and chilli powder, and cook for 3 minutes until browned. Stir in the soy sauce and stock, bring to the boil and simmer for 5 minutes.

2 Blend the cornflour with 1 tbsp of water until smooth, add to the pan and stir until slightly thickened. Season and stir in the basil.

Serve with boiled rice

Peppered beef

Black pepper stir-fry sauce can usually be found in the oriental section of the supermarket but if it's not available, or you prefer a milder flavour, use a sachet of hoisin or oyster sauce instead.

- Serves 2 (easily multiplied)
- Ready in 20 minutes
- Not suitable for freezing

1 tbsp sesame seeds
1 tbsp sunflower oil
1 large carrot, cut into matchsticks
160g mushrooms, sliced
1 lean rump steak, cut into strips
2 cloves of garlic, sliced
handful of mangetout, halved
150g sachet black pepper stir-fry sauce

1 Tip the sesame seeds into a large pan or wok and heat without oil until toasted. Tip onto a plate.

2 Heat the oil in the wok and stir-fry the carrots and mushrooms for a few minutes until almost cooked. Add the steak, garlic and mangetout, and continue cooking until the meat changes colour. It's better to undercook rather than overcook it. Toss in the sauce, and cook a few minutes more. Scatter over the toasted seeds.

Serve with noodles or rice

Sizzling salmon with honey and lime

Salmon is ideal for a quick after-work supper when you're short of time (trout fillets would work well too). This sauce would also be good with chicken, although it will take longer to cook under the grill.

■ Serves 4
■ Ready in 10 minutes
■ Not suitable for freezing

4 skinless salmon fillets
grated rind and juice of 1 lime
3 tbsp clear honey
1 tbsp wholegrain mustard

1 Turn on the grill to medium and put the salmon fillets slightly spaced apart in a shallow, heatproof dish.

2 Stir the lime rind and juice with the honey, mustard and a generous sprinkling of salt. Pour the mixture over the salmon and grill, without turning, for 5–6 minutes until the salmon is cooked all the way through.

Serve with potatoes and salad

Speedy beef stir-fry

It's hard to believe that a recipe with so few ingredients can taste so good! It works with strips of chicken instead of beef too, and you can even make a vegetarian version using chopped veg and a couple of handfuls of beansprouts.

■ Serves 4
■ Ready in 10 minutes
■ Not suitable for freezing

2 tbsp vegetable oil
400g beef strips or steak, cut into thin strips
1 red chilli, deseeded and finely sliced
2 tbsp soy sauce
handful of fresh basil leaves

1 Heat a wok or a large frying pan until smoking hot. Pour in the oil and swirl around in the pan, then tip in the beef strips and chilli. Cook for about 3 minutes, stirring all the time, until the meat is lightly browned, then pour over the soy sauce. Cook until heated through and the sauce coats the meat. Top with the basil leaves.

Serve with plain rice

easy
LOW-FAT MEALS
healthier – but just as tasty

Even if we're not following a strict, calorie-counted diet, most of us are aware that we should try to eat less fat if we want to stay fit and healthy – so we have an ongoing series in the magazine called 'Low fat ... but you'd never guess', full of recipes that contain 12g of fat or less, which are still packed with flavour.

There are two kinds of food that are usually a no-no when you're watching your fat intake ... Fried food is one of them, but our *Spice and lime chicken*, for example, gets round this with a 10-minute marinade that has enough oil in it already, without the need to add extra to the pan when you're cooking.

Curries, particularly take-aways, can be high in fat because the meat is often fried first and then coated in an oily sauce. But our clever *Fragrant chicken curry with chickpeas* uses no added oil – it still tastes wonderful and can be made in less time than it takes for a take-away curry to be delivered!

Ingredients like grilled chicken or lean steak are certainly low in fat but they can also be really boring. With a few simple tricks, though, you can jazz them up and turn them into something yummy. Take the *Chargrilled steak with orange and mustard vegetables* in this chapter, for example – the dressing on the veg gives the whole dish a real zing.

You'll also find a guilt-free alternative to chip-shop fish and chips, and a tasty way to use that under-rated but often overcooked vegetable, the humble cabbage – it will convert even the most confirmed cabbage hater!

Guilt-free fish and chips

Once you've tried this homemade version, you'll never want to eat greasy shop-bought fish 'n' chips ever again. Homemade tartare sauce is really easy to make, and tastes much better than the sort you buy in jars too.

- Serves 2
- Ready in 45 minutes
- 373 kcals, 9g fat, 1g sat. fat a portion
- Not suitable for freezing

450g potatoes, peeled and cut into chips
1 tbsp olive oil, plus a little extra for
   brushing
2 white fish fillets
grated rind and juice of 1 lemon
small handful of fresh parsley
   leaves, chopped
1 tbsp capers, chopped
2 heaped tbsp 0% Greek yogurt

1 Turn the oven to fan 180C/conventional 200C/gas 6. Toss the potatoes in the oil. Spread over a baking sheet in an even layer and bake for 40 minutes until browned and crisp. Put the fish in a shallow dish, brush lightly with oil and season lightly. Sprinkle with half the lemon juice and bake for 15 minutes. After 10 minutes, sprinkle over a little of the parsley and the lemon rind.

2 Meanwhile, mix together the capers, yogurt, remaining parsley and lemon juice. Spoon into a small bowl to serve.

Cod fillets and pan-fried cabbage

If you don't have a microwave, you can cook the cod fillets under a medium grill for 8 minutes or until they flake easily with a fork. In step 1, continue to cook the cabbage in the pan for 5 minutes until tender when prodded with the tip of a knife.

- Serves 4
- Ready in 20 minutes
- 241 kcals, 11g fat, 5g sat. fat a portion
- Not suitable for freezing

25g butter
4 rashers streaky bacon, chopped
1 small Savoy cabbage, shredded
150ml vegetable stock
4 cod fillets, each about 140g in weight,
   skinned

1 Melt the butter in a pan, add the bacon and cook until crisp. Stir in the cabbage. Pour over the stock and cook, stirring for 3 minutes until the cabbage is almost tender. Transfer to a microwaveable, heatproof dish.

2 Lay the fish on top of the cabbage. Dot with the remaining butter and season. Cover with plastic film and microwave on High for 5 minutes, or until the fish is cooked.

Serve with boiled potatoes

Spice and lime chicken

Using a tangy marinade like this means you don't need to add extra oil to cook the chicken – just make sure the pan is very hot before you start. This recipe works well with lamb leg steaks too.

- Serves 4
- Ready in 15 minutes
- 221 kcals, 5g fat, 1g sat. fat a portion
- Not suitable for freezing

150ml tub natural yogurt
1 tbsp vegetable oil
1 tsp medium curry powder or paste
pinch of chilli powder
juice of 1 lime
1 clove of garlic, crushed
4 skinless, boneless chicken breasts
1 red pepper, deseeded and cut into chunks
1 onion, halved and cut into large chunks

1 In a large bowl, mix together the yogurt, oil, curry powder or paste, chilli powder, lime juice and garlic. Season. Add the chicken and veg, and stir to coat. Cover and leave for 10 minutes.

2 Meanwhile, heat a griddle or frying pan until very hot and cook the chicken and veg for 8 minutes, turning the chicken after 4 minutes and ensuring it's cooked through.

Serve with rice, ready-made raita and plain naan bread

Spiced bean pilaf

You'll usually find bulgar wheat with the lentils and dried beans in the supermarket. It adds extra flavour, but you can make this with quick-cook rice if you have some in the cupboard already.

- Serves 4
- Ready in 30 minutes
- 248 kcals, 5g fat, 1g sat. fat a portion
- Not suitable for freezing

200g bulgar wheat
1 tbsp olive oil
1 large red onion, sliced
1 large courgette, roughly chopped
3 cloves of garlic, crushed
2 tsp cumin seeds, lightly crushed
1 tsp turmeric
200g runner beans, trimmed and sliced
140g cherry tomatoes
350ml vegetable stock
small handful of fresh coriander,
**   roughly chopped**

1 Cook the bulgar wheat in water for 15 minutes. Meanwhile, heat the oil in a large frying pan and cook the onion and courgette over a low heat for 5 minutes until soft. Stir in the garlic, cumin seeds and turmeric, and cook for 2 minutes, stirring occasionally.

2 Stir in the beans, tomatoes and stock, bring to the boil, cover and simmer for 6 minutes until the tomatoes are losing their shape.

3 Drain the bulgar wheat, stir into the vegetables and cook over a high heat for 2 minutes. Season and then stir in the fresh coriander.

Turkey minestrone

If you're roasting a turkey or a chicken for Sunday lunch, don't throw away the carcass. Put it in the fridge, covered, as soon as it's cooled and you've got the key ingredient for this tasty soup to make the next day.

■ Serves 8
■ Ready in 20 minutes, plus 1 hour to make the stock
■ 221 kcals, 9g fat, 2g sat. fat a portion
■ Not suitable for freezing

1 turkey or chicken carcass
800g mixed vegetables, such as carrots, leeks, celery, parsnips
2 bay leaves
4 cloves of garlic, peeled
1 large onion, quartered
handful of fresh parsley
4 tomatoes, diced
2 potatoes, diced
2 tbsp tomato purée
100g spaghetti, broken into small pieces, or other small pasta shapes
140g frozen peas
5 tbsp fresh pesto sauce
4 tbsp freshly grated parmesan

1 Break up the turkey carcass so it will fit into a very large pan. Take about two-thirds of the vegetables, cut into large chunks, and add to the pan with the bay leaves, garlic, onion, parsley and some seasoning. Pour over about 4 litres of cold water, bring to the boil, then cover and simmer gently for 1 hour.

2 Strain the stock into a clean pan (you need about 2.8 litres – freeze any excess for another time), reserving the carcass. Dice the rest of the vegetables and add to the pan with the tomatoes, potatoes and tomato purée. Simmer gently for 5 minutes, then tip in the pasta and cook for a further 10 minutes.

3 When the carcass is cool enough to handle, strip off any meat and add to the pan. Stir in the peas and pesto, then simmer for a few minutes until piping hot. Check the seasoning and adjust if necessary. Ladle into bowls and sprinkle with the parmesan.

Thai squash and pineapple

Coconut milk is an essential ingredient in Thai cooking, and we've used a low-fat version to get the same creamy effect in this vegetarian recipe. You can add extra veg like peas or broad beans, if you like.

- Serves 4
- Ready in 40 minutes
- 172 kcals, 9g fat, 5g sat. fat a portion
- Suitable for freezing

1 tbsp vegetable or sunflower oil
1 onion, chopped
4 tsp Thai red curry paste
1 medium butternut squash, peeled, deseeded and cut into chunks
half a 400ml can reduced-fat coconut milk
200ml vegetable stock
140g frozen green beans
237g can pineapple chunks in natural juice, drained
few fresh coriander leaves, to sprinkle

1 Heat the oil in a wok or pan. Fry the onion for 5 minutes until softened. Stir in the red curry paste, then add the squash, coconut milk and stock. Simmer for 15 minutes until the squash is tender. After 10 minutes cooking, tip in the green beans.

2 Stir in the pineapple and cook for just a few minutes until the pineapple heats through. Sprinkle with the coriander leaves.

Serve with rice or naan bread

Fragrant chicken curry with chickpeas

Curry can be high in fat, but by making a paste with the ingredients we've avoided frying and used no oil – so you get all the flavour, but much less fat.

- Serves 4
- Ready in 10 minutes, plus 30 minutes cooking
- 272 kcals, 5g fat, 1g sat. fat a portion
- Suitable for freezing

2 onions, quartered
3 cloves of garlic
3cm piece fresh root ginger, peeled and roughly chopped
2 tbsp medium curry powder
½ tsp turmeric
2 tsp paprika
1 red chilli, deseeded and roughly chopped
20g pack fresh coriander
1 chicken stock cube
4 skinless, boneless chicken breasts, cubed
410g can chickpeas, drained and rinsed

1 Tip the onions, garlic, ginger, spices, chilli and half the coriander into a food processor. Add 1 tsp of salt and blend to a purée. Tip the mixture into a medium saucepan and cook over a low heat for 10 minutes, stirring frequently.

2 Crumble in the stock cube, add 425ml of boiling water and return to the boil. Add the chicken, stir, then lower the heat and simmer for 20 minutes until the chicken is tender.

3 Chop the remaining coriander, reserve 2 tbsp, then stir the rest into the curry with the chickpeas. Heat through, divide among the bowls, and sprinkle with the reserved coriander.

Quick turkey curry

Don't save turkey just for Christmas – it makes a delicious change from chicken for weeknight meals, and is low in fat. You can vary the flavour of this depending on the curry paste you use – try a Thai green or korma curry paste, for example.

- Serves 4
- Ready in 25 minutes
- 292 kcals, 5g fat, 1g sat. fat a portion
- Not suitable for freezing

2 onions, thinly sliced
4 tbsp vegetable oil
2 tbsp Madras curry paste
425ml turkey or chicken stock
400g cooked turkey, cut into chunks
400g can chickpeas, drained

1 Fry half the onion in 2 tbsp of the oil for 6 minutes or until softened. Stir in the curry paste and cook for 2 minutes, then add the stock, turkey and chickpeas, and stir well. Bring to the boil, then simmer uncovered for 15 minutes until the turkey is thoroughly reheated and the sauce has thickened slightly.

2 Meanwhile, heat the remaining 2 tbsp of oil in a separate pan until very hot. Add the rest of the onion and fry quickly over a high heat until crisp and brown. Drain on kitchen paper.

Serve with basmati rice, a spoonful of natural yogurt and the crispy onions on top

Seafood tagliatelle

Using a bag of mixed seafood makes this really easy. You can buy it fresh or frozen from most supermarkets (it's sometimes called 'seafood cocktail'). If you're using frozen, defrost according to pack instructions and drain well before adding to the pan.

- Serves 4
- Ready in 25 minutes
- 469 kcals, 10g fat, 3g sat. fat a portion
- Not suitable for freezing

350g tagliatelle
100g diced bacon pieces
splash of olive oil
100g frozen broad beans
400g bag mixed seafood
good handful of rocket leaves
squeeze of fresh lemon juice

1 Cook the tagliatelle according to pack instructions, then drain.

2 Meanwhile, fry the bacon pieces in the oil until crisp. Add the broad beans and cook for 5 minutes until slightly softened. Tip in the seafood and cook for just 2 minutes. Toss in the tagliatelle and rocket. Season and add a squeeze of lemon juice.

Serve with a green salad and crusty bread

Chargrilled steak with orange and mustard vegetables

Lean steaks are great if you're following a low-fat diet – just be sure to cook them only briefly so they don't toughen in the pan. Orange juice, mustard and honey make a delicious combination for a sauce to go with them.

- Serves 4
- Ready in 25 minutes
- 317 kcals, 7g fat, 2g sat. fat a portion
- Suitable for freezing

450g new potatoes, halved lengthways
350g broccoli florets
finely grated rind and juice of 2 oranges
2 cloves of garlic, crushed
1 tbsp wholegrain mustard
2 tbsp clear honey
2 small orange peppers, deseeded and cut into chunks
4 lean, thin frying steaks
1 tsp vegetable oil

1 Cook the potatoes in boiling water for 6 minutes. Add the broccoli and return to the boil, cook for 3 minutes, or until tender, and drain well. Put the orange rind and juice in the empty pan, with the garlic, mustard and honey. Bring to the boil. Add the peppers. Cook on a high heat for about 2 minutes until the juices start to thicken. Add the vegetables and keep warm.

2 Heat a griddle pan or frying pan. Brush the steaks with the oil and season. If using a griddle, press the steaks down with a fish slice, so you get the chargrilled pattern. Cook for 2 minutes, turn over and cook for a further 2 minutes.

Serve with the vegetables and pan juices

Chicken, chickpea and lemon casserole

Nothing beats a warming casserole on a cold day, but they do tend to be high in calories and fat – and take a long time to cook. Our version is much healthier, and can be on the table in under an hour.

■ Serves 2
■ Ready in 40 minutes
■ 310 kcals, 6g fat, 1g sat. fat a portion
■ Suitable for freezing

175g small potatoes, halved
1 onion, thinly sliced
2 slices lemon, chopped
2 cloves of garlic, roughly chopped
1 tsp ground cumin
1 tsp ground cinnamon
450ml chicken stock
2 large skinless, boneless chicken thighs,
    trimmed of all fat and cut into cubes
half a 410g can chickpeas
handful of fresh coriander, chopped

1 Put the potatoes, onion, lemon and garlic into a casserole or heavy saucepan. Sprinkle over the ground spices and season lightly. Toss together then pour over the stock. Bring to the boil and simmer for 12 minutes or until the potatoes are tender.

2 Add the chicken and chickpeas, cover the saucepan and simmer gently for a further 12 minutes or until the chicken is cooked through. Check the seasoning and stir in the coriander.

Serve with steamed green beans or broccoli

easy
STANDBY
speedy meals with storecupboard ingredients

There are certain ingredients that we consider to be storecupboard essentials at *Easy Cook*, because they can be used as the basis for lots of different recipes at a moment's notice.

Take a jar of passata. Passata is sieved tomatoes, and it's a staple Italian ingredient. In this chapter, we've used it in the topping for a pizza (and it's great in place of a ready-made tomato pasta sauce too – add a teaspoon of sugar and any other ingredients you like, such as fried onions and garlic). Keep some in the cupboard as an emergency standby, and if you happen to have any left in the jar, simply decant it into a plastic container and freeze it (it will be fine for up to 3 months).

Talking of pizzas, you can't beat a ready-made pizza base – the kind you find near the dried pasta in the supermarket. In this chapter, we show you how you can add a roast vegetable or spicy Puttanesca topping in the time it would take to dial out for a take-away!

Flour tortillas are great too – you'll find two Latin-American inspired recipes to tempt you here, both of which are ideal if you've got a crowd to feed – the quantities are easy to scale up. The *Cajun chicken fajitas* work especially well – just put everything on the table and let everyone help themselves.

Red onion and feta pizza

We've used a fresh pizza base with a basic margherita topping – the sort you find in the supermarket chiller or freezer cabinet – and turned it into something special. You could make this with a storecupboard pizza base instead, and make your own topping from scratch with a jar of passata and some grated cheddar.

■ STANDBY INGREDIENT: two fresh cheese and tomato pizzas
■ Serves 4
■ Ready in 20 minutes
■ Not suitable for freezing

2 thin-crust cheese and tomato pizzas
1 small red onion, halved and thinly sliced
200g pack feta
160g cherry tomatoes, halved
grated rind of a lemon
½ tsp dried oregano

1 Turn the oven to the temperature recommended on the pizza packet. Unwrap the pizzas, place them on baking sheets, then scatter over the onion, crumble over the cheese and top with the tomatoes, lemon rind and oregano.

2 Cook according to pack instructions (about 12 minutes), until golden.

Serve with a bag of salad and your favourite dressing

Cajun chicken fajitas

As well as these two recipes, you can use flour tortillas whenever you fancy a change from bread or sandwiches – use them to roll up virtually anything, from sausages and mustard for breakfast to cheese and salad for a packed lunch. We love them!

- ▨ STANDBY INGREDIENT: flour tortillas
- ▨ Serves 2
- ▨ Ready in 20 minutes
- ▨ Not suitable for freezing

2 skinless chicken fillets, cut into strips
2 tbsp sunflower oil
2 tsp cajun spice seasoning
1 red onion, chopped
1 yellow pepper, deseeded and sliced
4 flour tortillas
4 handfuls of rocket salad
4 tbsp soured cream

1 Mix the chicken with half the oil and the spice seasoning. Heat the remaining oil in a wok or large frying pan and fry the onion and pepper until softened. Add the chicken to the pan and cook for about 5 minutes until tender.

2 Warm the tortillas then serve with the spicy chicken, salad, soured cream and some lime wedges, if you like.

Mexican pancakes

You can prepare this up to a day ahead if it's more convenient, then bake it when you're ready. Instead of the flour tortillas, you could also use ready-made pancakes from the chiller cabinet.

- ▨ STANDBY INGREDIENT: flour tortillas
- ▨ Serves 4
- ▨ Ready in 20 minutes, plus 25 minutes in the oven
- ▨ Suitable for freezing (unbaked)

2 red onions, cut into wedges
3 peppers, deseeded and sliced
1 fresh red chilli, deseeded and sliced
2 tbsp olive oil
220g can chopped tomatoes
20g pack fresh coriander, chopped
175g cheddar (a third diced, the rest grated)
8 small flour tortillas
215g can spicy refried beans
200ml tub crème fraîche

1 Fry the onions, peppers and half the chilli in the oil until almost tender. Add the tomatoes and half the coriander, and cook for 2 minutes more. Turn the oven to fan 170C/conventional 190C/gas 5.

2 Scatter the diced cheese on the tortillas with the pepper mix and beans. Roll up like pancakes and arrange them seam-side down in a large, shallow ovenproof dish.

3 Mix the grated cheese with the crème fraîche, remaining coriander and chilli. Spread over the pancakes and bake for 30 minutes until bubbling and golden.

Serve with a tomato and avocado salad

Roast vegetable pizza

A plain pizza base is a wonderful thing
to have in the cupboard for emergencies!
Look out for bases, which will keep in
the cupboard for months, in the same
aisle as dried pasta in the supermarket.
We've used passata as the base for our
topping – it comes in jars and is usually
sold alongside the canned tomatoes.

▓ STANDBY INGREDIENT: storecupboard
ready-made pizza base
▓ Serves 2
▓ Ready in 25 minutes
▓ Not suitable for freezing

2 red peppers, deseeded and cut into rings
1 leek, sliced
1 tsp olive oil
1 ready-made pizza base
4 tsp passata
125g pack mozzarella, drained and
   thinly sliced
12 cherry tomatoes
3 tbsp frozen peas
2 tbsp freshly grated parmesan

1 Turn the oven to fan 200C/conventional
220C/gas 7. Mix the peppers and leek in
the oil with some seasoning. Spread over a
baking sheet and roast for 10 minutes.

2 Spread the pizza base with the passata.
Scatter over the leek and peppers.
Arrange the cheese over the veg, scatter over
the cherry tomatoes and peas, then sprinkle
with parmesan.

3 Bake for 10 minutes until the crust is
crisp and lightly browned.

Pizza puttanesca

For this recipe, we've used a pasta
sauce for our topping – so in fact we're
making the most of two useful standby
ingredients in one recipe. It's a great
way to use up any sauce left over in a jar
from the night before, too.

▓ STANDBY INGREDIENT: storecupboard
ready-made pizza base
▓ Serves 2
▓ Ready in 15 minutes
▓ Not suitable for freezing

1 ready-made pizza base
4 tbsp tomato and chilli sauce from a jar
1 clove of garlic, sliced
3 anchovies in olive oil, drained
8 pitted black and green olives
½ tsp capers, drained and rinsed
50g sun-dried tomatoes, drained
small handful of fresh basil leaves

1 Turn the oven to fan 200C/conventional
220C/gas 7. Put the pizza base on a
baking sheet and spread with the sauce.
Scatter with the garlic, anchovies, olives,
capers and tomatoes.

2 Bake for 10 minutes or until the base is
cooked. Scatter with the basil.

Serve drizzled with a little chilli oil, if you like

Cheesy tortellini

Although fresh pasta sauces that you store in the fridge are a really useful standby, make sure you have a jar or two of pasta sauce in the storecupboard too – they will keep for months, so you'll always have the starting point for a quick and easy midweek supper.

- STANDBY INGREDIENT: jar of pasta sauce
- Serves 2 (easily doubled)
- Ready in 10 minutes
- Not suitable for freezing

250g pack large tortellini (we used spinach and ricotta)
100g ball mozzarella, torn into chunks
half a 400g jar tomato pasta sauce
drizzle of basil oil (optional)

1 Turn the grill to high. Splash a little cold water into a baking dish, then lay the tortellini in the dish in a single layer. Scatter half the mozzarella over the tortellini, spoon the sauce over, then top with the rest of the cheese.

2 Put the dish under the grill as high as possible and cook for 8 minutes until bubbling. Remove from the grill and drizzle over the basil oil, if using.

Serve with a green or tomato and onion salad

Ham and crème fraîche tart

The ready-made pastry you can buy these days is so good there's really no need to spend time making your own. The technique of marking a border with a knife and then adding a filling is a great one to know – the pastry rises up around the edges to form an instant, foolproof case. In this recipe, add half a tablespoon of wholegrain mustard to the crème fraîche before spreading it over the pastry, if you like.

▪ STANDBY INGREDIENT: pack of ready-rolled pastry
▪ Serves 4
▪ Ready in 20 minutes
▪ Not suitable for freezing

375g pack ready-rolled puff pastry
1 egg, beaten
100ml crème fraîche
8 slices cooked ham
handful of fresh flat-leaf parsley, chopped

1 Turn the oven to fan 200C/conventional 220C/gas 7. Put the pastry on a greased baking sheet and, using a sharp knife, score a line about 3cm inside to create a border. With a fork, prick the base inside the border only and brush over with the beaten egg.

2 Bake the pastry for 12 minutes until well risen. Spread the crème fraîche within the pastry border, season and then return to the oven for a further 8 minutes.

3 Remove the tart from the oven, then drape over the ham and sprinkle with the parsley.

Serve with a tomato and onion salad

Creamy leek, ham and cheese pasta

Save time by using a fresh ready-made pasta sauce, jazz it up with extra ingredients for this twist on a traditional pasta bake – and it can be on the table in about 15 minutes.

▪ STANDBY INGREDIENT: tub of fresh pasta sauce
▪ Serves 4
▪ Ready in 15 minutes
▪ Not suitable for freezing

250g fusilli
1kg leeks, sliced
300g tub fresh Fiorentina pasta sauce
100g ham, torn into strips
100g mature grated cheddar

1 Cook the pasta according to pack instructions, adding the leeks for the last 4 minutes of cooking time.

2 Meanwhile, turn on the grill to medium and heat the sauce in the microwave or according to pack instructions. Drain the pasta and leeks, return them to the pan and stir in the sauce and ham. Spoon the mixture into a shallow ovenproof dish and sprinkle with the grated cheddar. Grill for 5 minutes until bubbling and golden.

Serve with garlic bread and a green salad

easy everyday food

57

EASY STANDBY

Speedy Moroccan meatballs

You can buy ready-toasted almonds or you can toast them yourself while the meatballs are cooking – simply dry-fry them in a separate pan, stirring them around so they don't burn.

■ STANDBY INGREDIENT: pack of ready-made meatballs
■ Serves 4
■ Ready in 20 minutes
■ Suitable for freezing

350g pack ready-made beef meatballs (we used Swedish meatballs)
1 tbsp olive oil
1 onion, sliced
100g dried apricots, halved
1 small cinnamon stick
400g can chopped tomatoes with garlic
25g toasted flaked almonds
handful of fresh coriander, roughly chopped

1 Fry the meatballs in the oil for 10 minutes, turning occasionally until cooked. Remove from the pan. Add the onion and cook for a further 5 minutes, until soft.

2 Add the apricots, cinnamon and tomatoes. Half fill the empty can with water and add to the pan, then bring to the boil and simmer for 5 minutes. Remove the cinnamon. Return the meatballs to the pan and coat with the sauce. Sprinkle over the almonds and coriander.

Serve with couscous

Sausage meatballs with pasta

A pack of sausages is a useful standby to have in the fridge in its own right – but squeeze the sausage meat from the skins, and you have a whole new range of possibilities.

■ STANDBY INGREDIENT: pack of sausages
■ Serves 4
■ Ready in 20 minutes
■ Not suitable for freezing

400g penne
6 fat sausages
2 tbsp olive oil
2 x 250g bags spinach
4 tbsp pine nuts, toasted
85g parmesan, grated

1 Cook the pasta according to pack instructions. Meanwhile, squeeze the sausages from their skins, then roughly break the meat into 24 pieces. Roll into balls.

2 Heat the oil in a large frying pan, add the sausage balls, then cook over a medium heat until golden (about 5 minutes). Pile the spinach on top of the sausage balls and cook, stirring frequently, for 2–3 minutes until completely wilted. Season with a little salt and plenty of ground black pepper, then toss in the toasted pine nuts.

3 Add the drained pasta to the sausages and spinach, then toss well with half the parmesan. Serve spooned into individual serving bowls, with the rest of the parmesan scattered on top.

easy
FAMILY FOOD
recipes to get everyone round the table

Remember the time, not that long ago, when it was the norm for the whole family to sit down and eat together every evening? Everyone got a chance to relax, to talk about their day – and to eat a proper meal. Now, it's rare for us all to be home at the same time and families tend to dine in relays – weeknight meal times have become refuelling pit-stops rather than something to linger over.

There's a lot to be said for eating a meal together at least every now and again, whoever's doing the cooking. Vegging out with supper on a tray in front of the TV can be bliss sometimes – but not every night. *Easy Cook* is packed with family supper ideas that are quick and easy to prepare, that don't take a lot of fussing over – and that will bring everyone to the table.

Try our *Cottage pie jackets*, for example – a twist on baked potatoes, they can be ready in just over half an hour. We've also got some great ideas for turning *Macaroni cheese* into something a bit more special and a recipe for *Pastitsio*, a tasty variation on moussaka using minced lamb as a change from the minced beef that most of us usually buy.

Or why not try an old favourite like *Chilli con carne*? Our recipe is already really easy, but as it tastes even better when it's reheated, make double the quantity and freeze half so that the next time you serve it, there's absolutely no effort involved at all!

Macaroni cheese

When you're cooking this recipe, why not make double the quantity of the cheese sauce and keep it in the fridge overnight, then reheat it the next day and use it as a creamy topping for baked potatoes.

- Serves 4
- Ready in 40 minutes
- Not suitable for freezing

25g butter, plus extra for greasing and frying
500g pack macaroni
25g plain flour
600ml milk
200g grated cheddar
good grating of fresh nutmeg
1–2 rounded tsp ready-made English
   mustard
1 bunch of spring onions, finely chopped

1 Turn the oven to fan 180C/conventional 200C/gas 6 and grease a 1.5 litre ovenproof dish with butter. Cook the macaroni according to pack instructions.

2 Tip the butter, flour and milk into a pan then heat, stirring all the time with a hand whisk, until the sauce is thick and smooth. Remove from the heat and stir in two-thirds of the cheddar. When it has melted, stir in the nutmeg and mustard, and season.

3 Warm a knob of butter in a pan and fry the spring onions until soft. Tip into the dish. Pour in the sauce, add the drained macaroni and stir. Scatter over the remaining cheese and bake in the oven for 30 minutes.

Serve with a tomato and onion salad and crusty bread

Try these variations
- Stir some chopped ham into the cheesy sauce just before pouring it over the macaroni.
- Boil a handful of frozen peas with the macaroni for the last 3 minutes of the cooking time.
- Use red leicester in place of the cheddar to give the sauce a lovely orange colour and a sharper taste.
- For a crunchy topping, mix some white or brown breadcrumbs with the reserved cheddar before sprinkling it over the top, or add a handful of flaked almonds.

Cottage pie jackets

This new twist on cottage pie can be made from scratch in about half an hour by using the microwave, or you can bake the potatoes in the oven for 1 hour at fan 180C/conventional 200C/gas 6 until tender. Hollow and fill them then return to the oven for 15 minutes.

- Serves 4
- Ready in 35 minutes
- Not suitable for freezing

4 large baking potatoes
1 large onion, chopped
1 tbsp olive oil
500g pack minced beef
1 heaped tbsp plain flour
2 tbsp Worcestershire sauce
4 tbsp tomato ketchup
1 beef stock cube, crumbled
splash of milk
generous knob of butter
85g grated cheddar

1 Cook the potatoes in the microwave on High for 20 minutes until tender all the way through. Meanwhile, fry the onion in the oil until soft. Add the mince and flour, mix well then stir in the Worcestershire sauce and ketchup, and stock cube with a mug of hot water. Simmer for 20 minutes, stirring frequently.

2 When the potatoes are cooked, halve them and scoop out the flesh into a bowl. Mash the potatoes with milk, butter and some seasoning. Put the shells in a baking dish and fill with the mince. Top with the mash then the cheese and grill until bubbling.

Serve with green vegetables, or baked beans and tomatoes

Beef and bean pie

Sliced potatoes make a great topping to the recipe and there's also a bit of a cheat's ingredient here too – a can of baked beans in the filling. The tomato sauce they're in adds a delicious richness to the pie.

- Serves 4
- Ready in 45 minutes
- Suitable for freezing

2 onions, chopped
2 tbsp sunflower oil
500g pack lean minced beef
2 tbsp Worcestershire sauce
2 tbsp tomato ketchup
1 vegetable stock cube
750g potatoes, thickly sliced (no need to peel)
415g can baked beans
85g grated cheddar

1 Fry the onions in the oil for 5 minutes until softened. Increase the heat, add the mince and cook for 5 minutes, stirring all the time. Stir in the Worcestershire sauce, ketchup and stock cube. Pour in a mug of water, then bring to the boil. Cover, reduce the heat and simmer for 15 minutes.

2 Meanwhile, boil the potatoes for about 12 minutes until tender. Drain. Turn on the grill to medium. Stir the baked beans into the mince and heat through. Tip into a 2.5 litre ovenproof dish and cover with the potato slices. Sprinkle over the cheese then grill for 5 minutes, until golden.

Serve with green vegetables like broccoli and peas

Sausage and pasta bake

Pasta bakes reheat really well, so they're ideal to prepare ahead (up to a day in advance) and then pop in the oven when the family is ready for supper. Alternatively, you could cook the bake and then freeze it – cool it completely, then cover the dish loosely with cling film and over-wrap with foil. Thaw overnight in the fridge or at room temperature for a couple of hours before reheating in the oven for 40 minutes.

- Serves 6
- Ready in 50 minutes
- Suitable for freezing

450g pack pork sausages
1 large onion, chopped
1 tbsp olive oil
2 carrots, grated
450ml vegetable stock (or use 300ml stock
**   and 150ml red wine)**
3 tbsp tomato purée
50g butter
50g plain flour
600ml milk
freshly grated nutmeg
500g pack rigatoni
200g fresh spinach
140g grated cheddar

1 Slit the sausages and remove the skins, then snip the meat into small pieces with scissors. Fry the onion in the oil for 5 minutes. Stir in the sausage meat and fry until lightly coloured. Add the carrot, stir in the stock, wine if using, tomato purée and some seasoning. Bring to the boil, then reduce the heat and simmer uncovered for 15 minutes.

2 Tip the butter, flour and milk into a pan then heat, stirring all the time with a hand whisk, until the sauce is thick and smooth. Add a good sprinkle of the grated nutmeg and simmer for 2 minutes, still stirring.

3 Cook the pasta according to pack instructions. Drain then add the spinach straight away so it wilts in the heat of the pasta. Tip half the pasta into a shallow ovenproof dish and shake to level. Spoon over the sausage sauce, then tip the remaining pasta on top. Pour the white sauce over and sprinkle with the cheddar.

4 Turn the oven to fan 170C/conventional 190C/gas 5 and bake for 30 minutes, until the top is golden brown. If you've made this ahead so you are cooking it cold, straight from the fridge, add an extra 10 minutes to the baking time.

Serve with a tomato and onion salad, or a leafy salad with Little Gem and watercress

Sausages with cranberry gravy

This is delicious served with mustard mash – boil 900g potatoes for 15 minutes or until soft. Drain them, then mash with 25g butter and a tablespoon of grainy mustard. You can also make a lighter version of the mash, using half potatoes and half swede.

- Serves 4
- Ready in 20 minutes
- Not suitable for freezing

25g butter
1 onion, thinly sliced
454g pack Lincolnshire sausages
300ml chicken stock
3 tbsp cranberry sauce

1 Melt the butter in a frying pan, add the onion and fry until soft. Add the sausages and fry for about 8 minutes, turning often until brown.

2 Pour the stock into the pan and stir in the cranberry sauce. Bring to the boil and bubble for 3–4 minutes until the gravy has thickened, then season.

Serve with mustard mash and green veg

Bacon and mushroom pasta

Using a tablespoon of the pasta cooking water in the sauce is a handy technique to know – the starch from the pasta helps to thicken the sauce slightly. You could add a handful of peas to the cooking water 3 minutes before the pasta is cooked, if you like, and if you're cooking for vegetarians, this is good even without the bacon.

- Serves 4
- Ready in 20 minutes
- Not suitable for freezing

400g penne
8 rashers streaky bacon, snipped into bite-sized pieces
250g pack chestnut mushrooms, sliced
4 tbsp pesto
200ml tub half-fat crème fraîche
handful of fresh basil leaves

1 Cook the pasta according to pack instructions. Drain, reserving a tablespoon of the cooking water.

2 Fry the bacon and mushrooms in the same pan for 5 minutes until golden. Tip the pasta and reserved water back into the pan and heat for 1 minute. Remove the pan from the heat, spoon in the pesto and crème fraîche and most of the basil, and stir to combine. Sprinkle with the remaining basil to serve.

Serve with crusty bread and salad

Chilli con carne

Cook this chilli ahead, tip it into a bowl and cool, then cover tightly with cling film. Refrigerate the chilli for up to 3 days or pour the cold sauce into a plastic container, seal tightly and freeze for up to 3 months. Defrost before reheating until bubbling hot. If the chilli seems too thick, add a splash of water.

■ Serves 4
■ Ready in 50 minutes
■ Suitable for freezing

1 large onion, chopped
1 tbsp sunflower oil
2 cloves of garlic, chopped
1 red pepper, deseeded and chopped
2 heaped tsp mild chilli powder
1 tsp ground cumin
500g pack lean minced beef
400g can chopped tomatoes
½ tsp dried oregano
2 tbsp tomato purée
1 beef stock cube
420g can red kidney beans, drained
    and rinsed

1 Fry the onion in the oil for 5 minutes until soft then stir in the garlic, red pepper, chilli powder and cumin. Fry for 5 minutes more.

2 Turn up the heat, add the mince and break it up with a wooden spoon. Keep stirring, until all the mince is brown. Make sure you keep the heat hot enough for the meat to fry and brown rather than stew.

3 Tip in the tomatoes, oregano and tomato purée. Crumble over the stock cube and stir in a can of water. Bring to the boil, cover and bubble gently for 20 minutes. Add a dash of water if the mixture starts to dry out.

4 Stir in the beans and bubble gently without the lid for 10 minutes, adding a little more water if it's looking too dry. Replace the lid, turn off the heat and leave to stand for 10 minutes before serving to allow the meat to soak up some of the liquid, making it meltingly tender.

Serve with rice, soured cream and a salad

Cheese and mustard-crusted cod

You can use this topping for chicken too: take 4 skinless chicken breast fillets and bash them with the base of a saucepan to make them thinner. Top with the cheesy mixture then cook in the oven for 15–20 minutes until the chicken is tender and the topping is golden.

■ Serves 4
■ Ready in 20 minutes
■ Not suitable for freezing

4 skinless cod fillets
175g mature cheddar, grated
2 tsp wholegrain mustard
4 tbsp single cream
2 tbsp snipped fresh chives or spring onions

1 Turn the oven to fan 170C/conventional 190C/gas 5. Season the fish and put in an ovenproof serving dish.

2 Mix the cheese and mustard with the cream and chives or spring onions and spread over each cod fillet. Bake for 15 minutes until the fish is cooked and the top is golden.

Serve with a tomato salad and new potatoes

Spicy bean burgers

Kids love burgers – and so do most adults – and by making your own, you know exactly what goes into them. These are meat-free, so they're great if you've got a vegetarian in the family.

■ Serves 2
■ Ready in 20 minutes
■ Not suitable for freezing

1 red onion, finely chopped
2 sticks of celery, finely chopped
½ red chilli, deseeded and finely chopped (optional)
2 tbsp olive oil
420g can red kidney beans
1 tsp ground cumin
1 slice of bread, coarsely grated
1 egg, beaten

1 Fry the onion, celery and chilli in half the oil for 5 minutes, until soft. Meanwhile, drain, rinse and mash the beans.

2 Stir the cumin into the veg, then tip into the beans with the bread, egg and plenty of seasoning to make a moist paste.

3 Heat the remaining oil in a non-stick frying pan. Spoon the mixture into the pan in two spoonfuls. Press into two burgers. Cook for 3 minutes, flip over and cook for 3 minutes more.

Serve in rolls with lettuce, and yogurt mixed with chopped coriander and tomato

Pesto chicken

Chicken and pesto are a match made in heaven; add a few leaves of baby spinach with the pesto, if you like, for extra texture. This is very good served with rosemary potatoes: put 300g new potatoes, halved if large, in the pan 5 minutes before the chicken. Cook, tossing frequently. Add the leaves from 2 rosemary sprigs, then follow the chicken recipe, turning the potatoes occasionally.

- Serves 2 (easily doubled)
- Ready in 20 minutes
- Not suitable for freezing

2 boneless chicken breasts, skin on
2 tbsp green pesto sauce
1 tbsp olive oil
1 tbsp milk

1 Loosen the skin from the chicken with your fingers, leaving it attached down one side. Spread half the pesto over the chicken flesh then pull the skin back over to cover. Season.

2 Fry the chicken, skin-side down, in the oil over a high heat for about 3 minutes until the skin is crisp. Turn over, reduce the heat, then cover the pan and cook for 10 minutes more until cooked through. Remove from the pan.

3 Add the remaining pesto sauce to the pan with the milk, let it bubble, then season.

Serve with the extra pesto and new potatoes or rosemary potatoes

Pesto and parma ham pizza

If you want to get ahead, you can keep the pizzas in the fridge before you bake them – make sure they'll fit first, though! The cold inhibits the growth of the yeast in them and they'll be quite happy in there for about 4 hours.

- Serves 6 (makes 2 pizzas)
- Ready in 20 minutes, plus 20 minutes in the oven
- Not suitable for freezing

2 x 290g packs pizza base mix
8 tbsp grated fresh parmesan
120g tub fresh green pesto
20 cherry tomatoes, quartered
400g can artichokes, drained and quartered
85g pack parma ham
400g pack mozzarella, sliced

1 Turn the oven to fan 200C/conventional 220C/gas 7 and grease two 28 x 38cm Swiss roll tins. Tip both packs of pizza base mix into a bowl, add half the parmesan then make up according to pack instructions (check that you use the right amount of warm water for two packs).

2 Cut the dough in half, then stretch each piece so it fits the tin. Push it right into the corners with damp or oiled fingers to stop the dough sticking to them.

3 Spread with the pesto, then top evenly with the tomatoes, artichokes, ham (tear each slice in half first) and both the remaining cheeses. Bake for 20 minutes until the base is golden.

Serve with a big salad

Pastitsio

This is a twist on a traditional Greek dish. It's a bit like moussaka and it uses minced lamb, which makes a change from minced beef and has a distinctly different flavour.

■ Serves 6
■ Ready in 1 hour, plus 25 minutes in the oven
■ Suitable for freezing

1 onion, chopped
2 cloves of garlic, chopped
2 tbsp olive oil
4 rashers smoked streaky bacon,
   cut into strips
225g minced lamb
1 small aubergine, chopped
400g can plum tomatoes
¾ tsp ground allspice
6 tbsp roughly torn fresh oregano or
   4 tsp dried
125ml red wine
225g pasta
100g grated parmesan
40g butter
40g plain flour
425ml pint milk
3 tbsp fresh white breadcrumbs

1 Fry the onion and garlic in the oil for 5 minutes until golden. Add the bacon and cook for 3 minutes until crisp, then add the lamb and keep stirring to break up the mince. Cook until browned. Add the aubergine and cook, stirring occasionally, for about 3 minutes. Stir in the tomatoes, half a teaspoon of the allspice, half the oregano, and the wine. Bring to the boil, then lower the heat, cover and simmer for 45 minutes or until the meat is very tender and the sauce has thickened. Season.

2 Cook the pasta according to pack instructions until just tender and drain well. Spread half of the pasta over the base of a shallow ovenproof dish. Set aside 4 tbsp of the parmesan, then sprinkle half of the remaining cheese over the pasta. Spoon half of the meat sauce evenly over the cheese, then repeat the layers with the remaining pasta, cheese and meat sauce. Turn the oven to fan 170C/conventional 190C/gas 5.

3 Put the butter, flour, milk and remaining allspice in a pan. Bring to the boil, whisking constantly, until the mixture is thickened and smooth, then simmer for 3 minutes. Season.

4 Pour the sauce evenly over the meat and pasta, making sure that all of it is covered. Mix the breadcrumbs with the reserved parmesan and the remaining oregano in a bowl. Sprinkle the mixture over the Pastitsio and bake for 25 minutes until bubbling.

easy
PUDS
for when you want something fast and sweet

For many of us, a meal just isn't a meal unless there's something sweet to round it off – but who's got the time, or the energy, to concoct a fancy dessert at the end of a busy weekday?

We've included plenty of our 10-minute puddings in this chapter, from *Quick peach brûlée*, which uses cupboard ingredients, to our magic *Instant raspberry ice*, which everyone should try because it's so simple and effective.

We've also included a couple of recipes, like the *Light rice pudding*, that take just a few minutes to prepare and then you can pop them in the oven and forget about them for a while.

Fruit is always good for a quick pud and we've used lots of it here, including fresh raspberries and strawberries. But only buy them in season – they're much more expensive and they don't taste anywhere near as good during the colder months. That doesn't mean you can't use fruit at all in the winter though – we're great fans of canned fruit when fresh isn't an option. And good old bananas are the ultimate convenience food because you can just peel and eat them but, better still, use them in our *Pineapple and banana custard meringues* and *Sticky banana waffles*.

If you've got friends coming over for a weeknight supper, you can't go wrong with our *Chocolate cherry trifle* – it's decadent and delicious, but only takes 20 minutes to prepare.

Rhubarb and strawberry meringue pots

If you're short of time, you can cook the rhubarb, sugar and rind in the microwave for 10 minutes on full power, stirring halfway through cooking time, until just tender.

- Serves 4
- Ready in 15 minutes, plus 1 hour in the oven
- Not suitable for freezing

450g rhubarb, cut into 4cm chunks
100g caster sugar
grated rind of 1 orange
1 tbsp strawberry conserve
2 eggs, separated

1 Turn the oven to fan 160C/conventional 180C/gas 4. Put the rhubarb in an ovenproof dish, sprinkle over 50g of the sugar and the orange rind, and stir together. Cover and bake in the oven for 35–40 minutes until tender.

2 Remove the rhubarb from the oven and allow to cool slightly. Stir in the conserve, then the beaten egg yolks. Divide the rhubarb mixture among four 175ml ramekins. Put on a baking sheet and cook in the oven for 10 minutes until lightly thickened.

3 While the rhubarb mixture is cooking, whisk the egg whites until stiff. Sprinkle over half of the remaining sugar and whisk again. Gently fold in the rest of the sugar. Pile the meringue on top of the rhubarb to cover it completely and swirl the top. Return to the oven for 10 minutes until the meringue is puffy and golden.

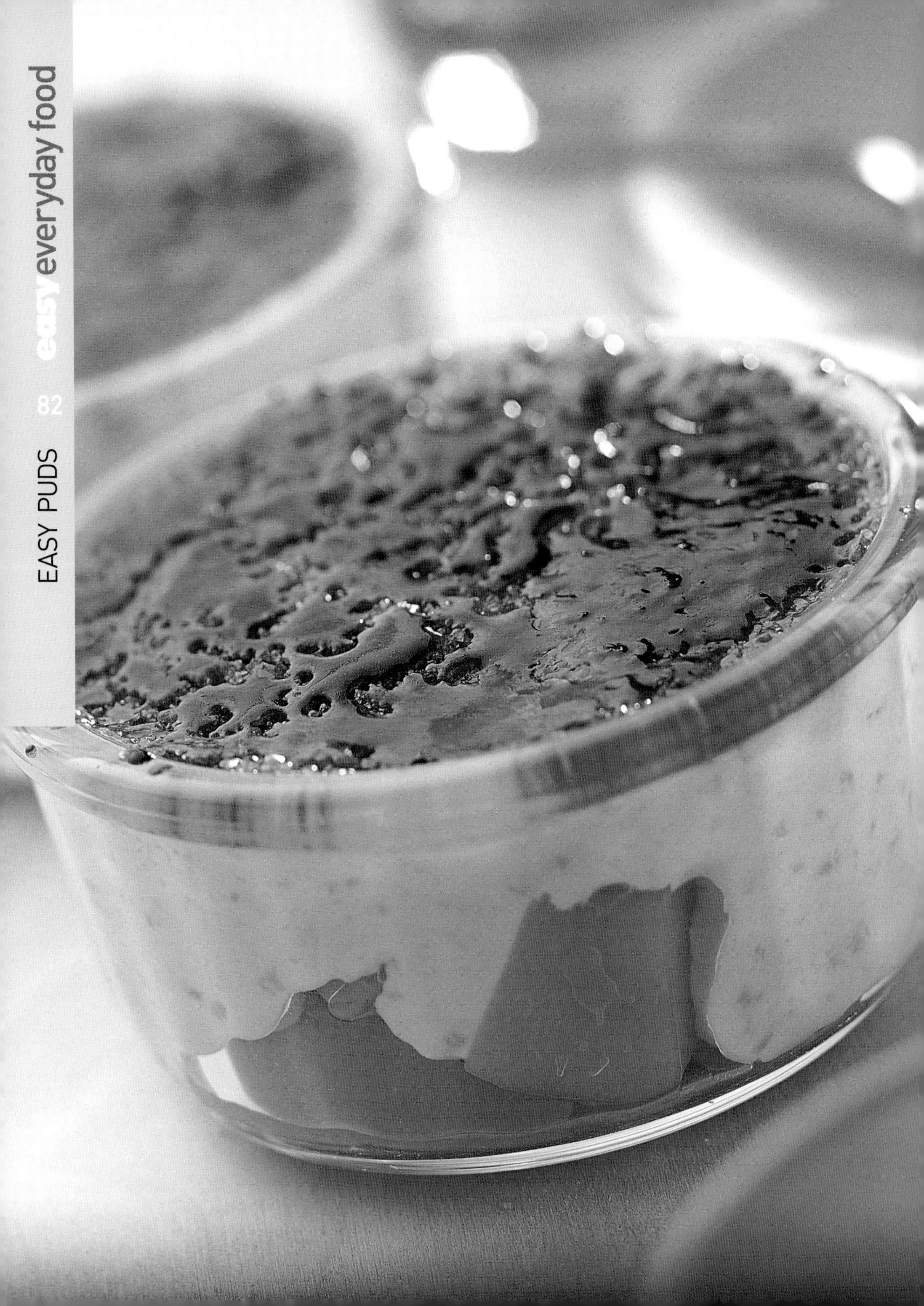

Quick peach brûlée

To give the topping a toffee flavour, you can use demerara instead of caster sugar, if you have some handy. You can vary the fruit you use too – apricots work especially well (either use them from a can, or poach fresh apricots in a little water until soft).

▓ Serves 4
▓ Ready in 10 minutes
▓ Not suitable for freezing

410g can peach slices in natural juice, drained
¼ tsp ground cinnamon
finely grated rind ½ an orange
425g can rice pudding
4 tbsp caster sugar

1 Turn on the grill to medium. Roughly chop the peaches, then put into four ramekins or heatproof cups.

2 Stir the cinnamon and orange rind into the rice pudding, then spoon over the peaches. Smooth the tops with the back of a spoon and sprinkle evenly with sugar. Grill for 5 minutes until the sugar has caramelized. Cool a little before eating as the sugar will be very hot.

Chocolate cherry trifle

If you're after a dessert that looks and tastes amazing but takes very little time to make, try this. It's a real cheat's recipe, but there's nothing wrong with that once in a while!

▨ Serves 8
▨ Ready in 20 minutes, plus setting time
▨ Not suitable for freezing

135g packet blackcurrant jelly, cubed
425g can pitted cherries
180g shop-bought madeira or chocolate
**   cake, diced**
568ml carton double cream
4 tbsp caster sugar
500g carton fresh custard
3 tbsp chocolate sauce

1 Put the jelly in a large Pyrex measuring jug with 3 tbsp of water and microwave on High for 1½ minutes until melted (follow the pack instructions if you don't have a microwave). Add the cherries and juice, then make up to 750ml with cold water. Tip the cake into a large serving bowl and pour the jelly mix on top.

2 Whip the cream and sugar until the cream holds its shape, but is not stiff. Fold a quarter in to the custard to make the custard consistency a little thicker, then drizzle in the chocolate sauce and stir very gently to marble it through the custard. Spoon onto the jelly then blob large spoonfuls of the cream on top to cover it. Chill for several hours or overnight to set the jelly.

Sticky banana waffles

This is a great year-round dessert, but you can also ring the changes by using fruits like strawberries or raspberries when they're in season. Vary the ice cream you use too – coffee ice cream goes very well with banana.

▨ Serves 1 (easily multiplied)
▨ Ready in 10 minutes
▨ Not suitable for freezing

2 waffles
2 scoops praline ice cream
1 banana, sliced
handful of pecan nuts, chopped
maple syrup or clear honey

1 Toast the waffles, then top with the ice cream and banana slices, and scatter over the pecan nuts. Drizzle over the maple syrup or honey and serve.

Tipsy berries

Don't leave this to soak for longer than the time it takes to eat your main course as alcohol draws the juice from strawberries and they tend to go a bit soggy if you leave them in the wine mixture for too long.

- Serves 6
- Ready in 10 minutes, plus marinating
- Not suitable for freezing

700g strawberries, hulled and halved
4 tbsp caster sugar
handful of fresh mint leaves
½ bottle red wine

1 Before you sit down to the meal, pile the strawberries in a serving bowl and scatter with the sugar and most of the mint. Pour over the red wine then leave until ready to eat. Scatter with the remaining mint as you bring it to the table.

Serve with some crisp biscuits like shortbread

Instant raspberry ice

This clever dessert is like magic as the frozen fruit makes an instant sorbet in minutes. You do need to eat it fairly quickly rather than freezing it for another day, though.

- Serves 4
- Ready in 10 minutes
- Not suitable for freezing

1 large ripe banana
3 tbsp caster sugar
squeeze of fresh lemon juice
340g pack frozen raspberries

1 Slice the bananas into a food processor and whizz with the sugar, lemon juice and raspberries until smooth but still icy. It will store in the freezer for about an hour.

Serve with shortbread

Hot strawberry sandwiches

This is a great way of using up leftover sliced bread. Fresh strawberries are the best fruit to use for this recipe because they are firm enough to slice for the filling, but will also quickly whizz to a purée for the sauce.

- Serves 4
- Ready in 25 minutes
- Not suitable for freezing

50g butter
8 slices white bread, crusts removed
225g strawberries, sliced
2 tbsp caster sugar
1 egg, beaten
3 tbsp milk

1 Spread a little butter around the edges of four slices of bread. Use two-thirds of the strawberry slices and all the bread slices to make four 'sandwiches' (one buttered and one unbuttered for each). Press the edges together to seal.

2 Whizz the remaining strawberries and half of the caster sugar in a food processor, or mash well with a potato masher.

3 Beat together the egg and milk in a wide, shallow bowl. Heat the remaining butter in a large frying pan and, when it's bubbling, quickly dip both sides of each sandwich in the egg and milk, then add to the pan. Cook on both sides until golden and crisp (you may need to do this in two batches). Put a sandwich on each plate, sprinkle with the remaining sugar and top with a drizzle of the strawberry sauce.

Serve with a scoop of vanilla ice cream

Light rice pudding

This rice pudding couldn't be easier to make – it pretty much cooks itself. Just pop it in the oven and forget about it while you get on with other things.

- Serves 4
- Ready in 2¼ hours
- Not suitable for freezing

100g short-grain or pudding rice
50g caster sugar
700ml semi-skimmed milk
pinch of grated fresh nutmeg
1 bay leaf or a strip of lemon rind

1 Turn the oven to fan 130C/conventional 150C/gas 2. Wash the rice and drain well. Butter an 850ml heatproof baking dish, then tip in the rice and sugar, and stir through the milk. Sprinkle the nutmeg all over and top with the bay leaf or lemon rind. Cook for 2 hours or until the pudding wobbles slightly when shaken.

Serve hot or cold with dried fruit or fruit compote

Pineapple and banana custard meringues

If you loved banana custard as a child, you should definitely try this new twist on the traditional recipe. Using a tub of fresh custard means it's really speedy to put together.

- Serves 4
- Ready in 20 minutes
- Not suitable for freezing

227g can pineapple pieces in natural juice
500g tub fresh half-fat custard
50g caster sugar
2 bananas, sliced
2 eggs, whites only

1 Turn the oven to fan 170C/conventional 190C/gas 5. In a medium-sized bowl, mix the pineapple and juice with the custard, half the sugar and the sliced bananas. Stir gently, then spoon into four individual baking dishes or large ovenproof teacups. Bake on a baking sheet for 5 minutes.

2 Meanwhile, whisk the egg whites until they hold their shape (use an electric hand whisk, if you have one). Tip in the remaining sugar and whisk until glossy. Pile onto the desserts and bake for 5 minutes more until golden brown and glossy.

Raspberry shortbread

When you're making shortbread, it's important to handle the dough as little as possible to keep it lovely and light. You can use strawberries instead of raspberries on top, if you prefer, and you can make the bases up to a week ahead and keep them in an airtight container.

- Serves 6
- Ready in 15 minutes, plus 12 minutes cooking
- Not suitable for freezing

100g butter
50g icing sugar, plus extra for dusting
½ tsp vanilla extract
175g self-raising flour
25g cornflour
1 egg yolk
200ml tub crème fraîche
225g fresh raspberries

1 Turn the oven to fan 160C/conventional 180C/gas 4. Cream together the butter, sugar and vanilla extract. Lightly mix in the flour and cornflour, then add the egg yolk to bind. To save time, do this in a food processor, if you have one.

2 Roll out the shortbread very thinly on a lightly floured surface and cut out using a 10cm-diameter cutter (the base of a bowl is good for this). Gather the trimmings and repeat until you have six discs. Put the discs on two ungreased baking sheets. Prick each disc several times with a fork and bake for 12 minutes until pale golden. Allow to cool, then transfer onto a wire rack to cool completely.

3 Spread the shortbread bases with crème fraîche and scatter over the raspberries. Dust with a little icing sugar.

PART TWO

easy weekend food

When you've got a little more time to spend in the kitchen, these recipes are perfect

Once the weekend comes around, there's a little more time to take a relaxed approach to cooking and you can experiment a bit and have some fun with recipes. In our 'Easy Weekend Food' section, we've come up with plenty of ways to help you do just that.

You'll find some great classic recipes, plus starters, main courses and puddings that are ideal for entertaining. Whether you've got in mind a supper with friends, a more formal dinner party (no one needs to know the recipes you've cooked are full of clever short-cuts!), or a Sunday lunch with the family, you'll find what you're looking for here.

You'll also find a selection of easy-to-make snacks to keep you going – and why not follow our suggestion to kick back from the normal weekend routine and, instead of starting the weekend with chores and shopping trips, take time out to enjoy a casual Saturday lunch with friends every once in a while?

easy
CLASSICS
traditional recipes made super-simple

There are certain recipes that every cook should have in their repertoire: recipes that have stood the test of time and that can be used regularly for all sorts of different occasions. In this chapter, we've brought together some of our all-time favourites – give them a try, and you'll find you will make your own personal favourites over and over again.

Our *Simple spaghetti bolognese* is top of the list. It takes just minutes to prepare and then simmers on the hob for half an hour until the meat is tender and the sauce has become thickened and delicious. Serve it the usual way, over a mound of spaghetti – or ring the changes and spoon it over potato gnocchi with a sprinkling of grated cheese. It makes a great base for a cottage pie, too.

If there's a vegetarian in the family, our *Vegetable chilli bowl* – a meat-free twist on the classic chilli con carne recipe – is ideal, and it's brilliant for feeding a crowd too as the ingredients are easily multiplied. *Chunky fish chowder* is

also a wonderfully versatile recipe. The quantities we've given serve four if you want to eat it as a main meal with a little crusty bread on the side – or put it in small bowls or even pretty tea cups to serve eight as a starter when friends come round.

At *Easy Cook*, you may have noticed by now that we love recipes that look impressive but are actually really simple to make – and *Lamb and rosemary parcels* are a great example. Take four lamb leg steaks, sprinkle with chopped rosemary and wrap in ready-rolled puff pastry with a spoonful of tangy cranberry sauce. What could be better – or easier?

Simple spaghetti bolognese

This is a can't-go-wrong version of a recipe that you'll want to make time and time again. You can also use the meat sauce as a base for lasagne, layered up with sheets of fresh pasta and cheese sauce either homemade or in a tub from the chiller cabinet.

■ Serves 4
■ Ready in 40 minutes
■ Suitable for freezing

2 tbsp olive oil
500g pack lean beef mince
1 rasher back bacon, chopped
1 onion, finely chopped
1 clove of garlic, finely chopped
75ml red wine
250ml beef stock
leaves from 2 thyme sprigs
1 small carrot, chopped
400g can plum tomatoes
1 tsp tomato purée (optional)
½ bunch of fresh basil
400g spaghetti

1 Heat 1 tbsp of the olive oil in a non-stick frying pan. When hot, tip in the mince and cook for 5 minutes until browned all over, breaking up any lumps with the back of a spoon. Tip onto a plate.

2 Add the bacon to the pan with the onions and garlic, then cook for 2 minutes until the bacon is crispy. Return the mince to the pan, pour in the red wine, stock and thyme leaves. Bring to the boil, then simmer for 30 minutes until the mince is tender and the sauce has reduced down, and season.

3 Meanwhile, heat the remaining tbsp of olive oil in a non-stick frying pan. Tip in the carrot and cook for 5 minutes to soften. Scoop the tomatoes from the can, reserving the juices. Add to the pan and cook for 5 minutes more. Pour over the reserved tomato juice, stir in the tomato purée, if using, and most of the basil, then simmer for 15 minutes. Whizz together in a blender until smooth.

4 Cook the spaghetti according to pack instructions. Drain, reserving a few tablespoons of the cooking water. Tip the spaghetti into the pan with the mince and add the tomato sauce. Thin with a little of the reserved water, if needed, then toss together.

Serve sprinkled with extra basil and toasted breadcrumbs, or grated parmesan

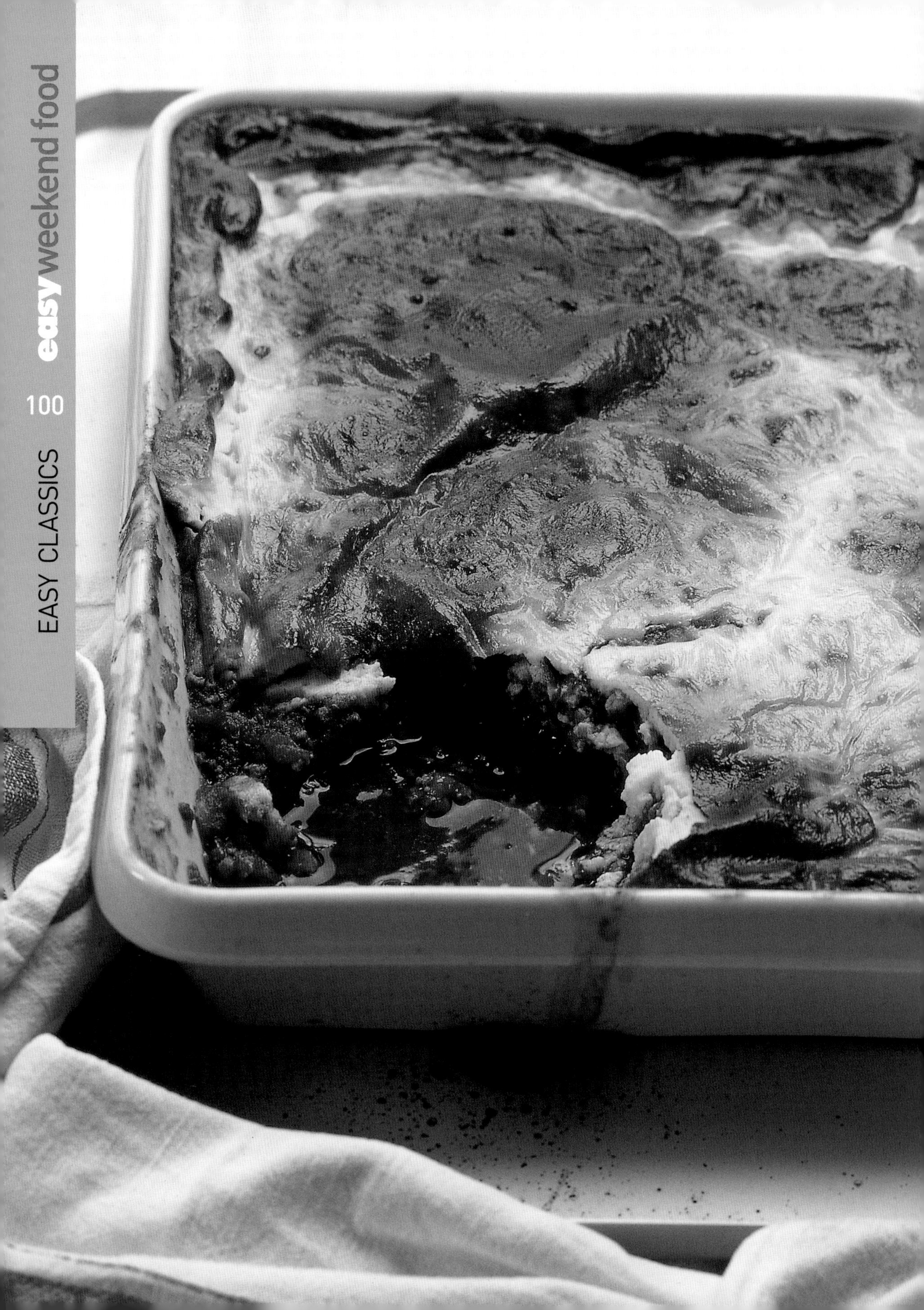

Cheat's moussaka

If you want to make this ahead, it will keep unbaked in the fridge overnight. Cool the mince before pouring on the yogurt topping, though, to keep the layers separate – if the mince is warm, the topping will start to melt into it.

■ Serves 4 generously
■ Ready in 40 minutes, plus 30 minutes in the oven
■ Suitable for freezing (cooked mince only)

1 large onion, chopped
1 tbsp olive oil
500g pack lamb or beef mince
2 tsp dried oregano
1 tsp ground cinnamon
2 x 400g cans chopped tomatoes
1 vegetable stock cube, crumbled
1 aubergine, cubed
1 large potato, peeled and cubed
500g pot natural yogurt
2 eggs
85g finely grated mature cheddar

1 Turn the oven to fan 160C/conventional 180C/gas 4. Fry the onion in the oil in a large pan for 5 minutes, stirring occasionally until soft. Add the mince and stir-fry until brown.

2 Sprinkle in the oregano and cinnamon, stir well then add the tomatoes with a can full of water, the stock cube and plenty of seasoning. Bring to the boil, stir in the aubergine and potato then cover and cook for 20 minutes until the veg are tender.

3 Mix the yogurt with the eggs and two-thirds of the cheddar. Tip the meat into an ovenproof dish, pour over the yogurt mixture and sprinkle with the rest of the cheese. Bake for 30 minutes until the topping is set and golden. Cool for 5 minutes before serving.

Serve with a tomato and onion salad and some crusty bread

Chicken noodle stir-fry

Adapt this recipe using whatever you have in the fridge. Add strips of carrot or broccoli florets, for example – or use pork or beef instead of chicken.

- Serves 2
- Ready in 15 minutes, plus 10 minutes cooking
- Not suitable for freezing

100g medium egg noodles
3 tbsp soy sauce
2 tbsp sherry
1 tbsp clear honey
2 boneless, skinless chicken breasts, sliced
3 tbsp sunflower oil
1 red and 1 yellow pepper, deseeded and sliced
thumb-sized piece fresh root ginger, peeled and cut into matchsticks
100g baby sweetcorn, sliced
100g mangetout, halved at an angle
220g can sliced bamboo shoots in brine, drained

1 Pour boiling water over the noodles, leave them to soak for 3 minutes, then drain and rinse with cold water to stop them sticking. Spoon the soy sauce, sherry and honey into a bowl and whisk with a fork.

2 Fry the chicken in 2 tbsp of oil in a wok or frying pan, stirring vigorously. Keep the strips constantly moving to separate them.

3 Tip in the peppers, the remaining oil, ginger and sweetcorn. Stir to mix, stir-fry for 4 minutes. Pour in the soy sauce mixture.

4 Tip in the mangetout, bamboo shoots, then the noodles, separating them with your fingers as you add them to the pan. Stir-fry for 2 minutes, until piping hot and everything is well mixed.

Chunky fish chowder

Use undyed smoked haddock for this, if you can find it in the supermarket – it's a much paler colour than the bright yellow dyed fish, but has a better flavour. This is a substantial soup that's a meal in itself.

- Serves 4
- Ready in 20 minutes
- Suitable for freezing

1 onion, thinly sliced
500g potatoes, peeled and cut into chunks
1.2 litres milk
1 clove of garlic, crushed
300g can sweetcorn kernels, drained
450g skinless smoked haddock
2 tbsp chopped fresh parsley

1 Put the onion and potatoes into a large saucepan, pour the milk over and season well with pepper. Bring to the boil, cover and simmer for 10 minutes, stirring occasionally.

2 Stir in the garlic, sweetcorn and fish, bring back to the boil, cover and simmer for 5 minutes. Flake the fish into bite-sized pieces with a fork. Stir in the chopped parsley and season.

Serve with crusty bread

Moroccan lamb meatballs

If you don't have paprika in the cupboard, you can use half a teaspoon of chilli powder instead. The meatballs are great served with couscous, but you could also serve them with pasta or even mashed potato, if you prefer.

■ Serves 4
■ Ready in 40 minutes
■ Suitable for freezing (meatballs only)

1 onion, chopped
1 clove of garlic, crushed
4 tbsp sunflower oil
1 tsp each ground cumin, ground coriander, paprika
450g lamb mince
400g can chopped tomatoes
300ml vegetable stock
grated rind of 1 lemon
handful of fresh coriander

1 Fry the onion and garlic in 2 tbsp of the oil for 4 minutes. Stir in the spices and cook for 1 minute. Cool. Mix half the mixture with the minced lamb and shape into 24 meatballs.

2 Fry the meatballs in the remaining oil until browned (you might need to do this in batches). Set aside. Add the remaining onion mixture to the pan with the chopped tomatoes and stock, return the meatballs and simmer for 30 minutes. Stir in the lemon rind and some fresh coriander.

Serve with couscous

Deep-filled steak pie

It takes just a few minutes to prepare the filling and then you can leave it to cook gently on the hob. The cooked pie can be frozen – defrost it in the fridge and reheat at fan 180C/conventional 200C/gas 6 for 40 minutes.

■ Serves 6
■ Ready in 10 minutes, plus 2 hours cooking
■ Suitable for freezing

2 onions, chopped
1 tbsp vegetable oil
700g braising steak, cubed
2 tbsp plain flour
600ml beef stock
2 bay leaves
leaves from 4 fresh thyme sprigs
4 flat mushrooms, thickly sliced
1 tsp tomato purée
1 egg, beaten
375g pack ready-rolled puff pastry

1 Fry the onions in the oil until softened. Add the meat and fry, stirring, for 3 minutes until browned. Stir in the flour and cook for 2 minutes, then pour in the stock and herbs. Stir until thickened and coming to the boil. Add the mushrooms and the tomato purée, lower the heat and simmer, covered, for about 1½ hours until the meat is tender.

2 When cooked, remove the bay leaves, season, then cool slightly. Tip into an ovenproof pie dish. Turn the oven to fan 180C/conventional 200C/gas 6.

3 Brush the rim of the dish with a little of the beaten egg, lay the pastry on top and press down to seal. Brush with a little more egg. Bake for 20 minutes or until golden.

Serve with mashed potatoes and green beans or peas

Vegetable chilli bowl

The classic recipe for chilli con carne lends itself surprisingly well to a meat-free version too. Kidney beans and mushrooms give just the right texture, and work beautifully with the spicy tomato sauce.

- Serves 4
- Ready in 20 minutes
- Suitable for freezing

2 cloves of garlic, crushed
2 red chillies, finely chopped
1 tbsp olive oil
2 tsp ground cumin
250g chestnut mushrooms, quartered
400g can chopped tomatoes
400g can red kidney beans, drained
150g fine green beans, trimmed

1 Fry the garlic and chilli in the oil for 2 minutes. Add the cumin and mushrooms and cook for 3 minutes. Add the tomatoes, kidney beans and 200ml of water, then stir and simmer for 10 minutes.

2 Add the green beans and cook for 5 minutes more, until the veg are tender and the sauce is thickened.

Serve with a spoonful of crème fraîche and crusty bread

Oven-baked mushroom and thyme risotto

A traditional risotto recipe can be off-putting, as you have to add hot stock a little at a time until it's all absorbed and it's tricky to judge when it reaches the right consistency. This recipe does away with all that – put it in the oven and 25 minutes later it will come out just right.

- Serves 4
- Ready in 30 minutes
- Not suitable for freezing

25g pack dried porcini mushrooms
2 tbsp olive oil
1 small onion, finely chopped
2 cloves of garlic, crushed
350g risotto rice
2 tsp fresh thyme leaves, plus extra to serve
750ml vegetable stock
100ml white wine
handful of freshly grated parmesan

1 Put the mushrooms in a bowl, pour over 425ml of boiling water and leave to soak for 10 minutes. Meanwhile, heat the oil in an ovenproof pan and fry the onion for 2 minutes until starting to soften. Add the garlic and cook for another minute.

2 Turn the oven to fan 170C/conventional 190C/gas 5. Drain the mushrooms, reserve the liquid, and chop. Add the rice, mushrooms and thyme to the pan, then stir well. Strain over the mushroom liquid, pour in the stock and wine, and bring to the boil.

3 Season, then bake for 25 minutes or until the rice is just cooked and all the liquid has been absorbed. Stir in the grated parmesan and sprinkle with extra thyme leaves and parmesan shavings.

Serve with a crispy salad

Lamb and rosemary parcels

Puff pastry and lamb go together really well and these smart little parcels are very tasty. They're a good way of using up a jar of cranberry sauce, if you have some in the fridge, too.

■ Serves 4
■ Ready in 30 minutes, plus chilling and 15 minutes in the oven
■ Suitable for freezing

4 boneless lamb leg steaks
3 fresh rosemary sprigs, stripped and chopped, plus 4 small sprigs
1 tbsp olive oil
375g pack ready-rolled puff pastry
4 tbsp cranberry sauce
1 egg, beaten

1 Turn the oven to fan 200C/conventional 220C/gas 7. Season the lamb and sprinkle with the chopped rosemary then brown in the oil for 3 minutes each side. Cool.

2 Cut the pastry into four rectangles and roll out each piece large enough to wrap a lamb steak. Put the lamb on the side of each one and top with a tbsp of cranberry sauce.

3 Brush the edges of the pastry with a little beaten egg, then fold them over the lamb and pinch the edges to seal them firmly. Put on a baking sheet and lightly cover with cling film until ready to cook. They will keep in the fridge overnight.

4 Brush the pastry with the beaten egg, push a small sprig of rosemary into each one and bake for 15 minutes, until risen and golden.

Serve with sauté potatoes and green veg

Bacon and mushroom meatloaf

If you have any of this left over, you can heat it in the microwave and serve in baps or rolls, with thinly sliced tomatoes, onion and a little mayonnaise.

■ Serves 4
■ Ready in 15 minutes, plus 50 minutes in the oven
■ Suitable for freezing

500g pack extra-lean beef mince
1 onion, finely chopped
1 egg
85g bread, coarsely grated or made into crumbs
150g button mushrooms, quite finely chopped
8 rashers smoked streaky bacon, chopped
½ beef stock cube
4 tbsp tomato ketchup
85g grated cheddar

1 Turn the oven to fan 160C/conventional 180C/gas 4. Tip the beef, onion, egg and breadcrumbs into a large bowl, with half the mushrooms and bacon. Crumble in the stock cube then spoon in the ketchup. Season really well, then thoroughly mix everything.

2 Press the mixture into a 1kg non-stick loaf tin and bake for 30 minutes. Mix the remaining bacon and mushrooms with the grated cheese to make a topping.

3 After 30 minutes, take the loaf from the oven. Pour off any liquid in the tin. Scatter over the topping and return to the oven for 20 minutes until golden. Cool for 5 minutes, then loosen the sides with a knife and turn it out from the tin. Serve cut into thick slices.

easy
SNACKS

feeling peckish? Rustle up one of these tasty ideas

There are times at the weekend when you want something quick and easy to fill you up, but you haven't got time to stand over a pan or fiddle about with lots of ingredients. The recipes in this chapter will fit the bill perfectly.

Some of them can be ready in a matter of minutes, like *Spinach and ham muffin*, *Salmon rarebit* (which uses canned salmon), *Cheese and pepper pitta pocket* and *Eggy bread*. The meat in our *Beefy ciabattas* tastes best if it's marinated for a couple of hours, so just pop it in the fridge before you go out to do your Saturday-morning shop, and it'll be ready to use by the time you come back. If you're making *Tomato and dolcelatte calzone*, they need 20 minutes in a warm place to rise (the airing cupboard is ideal) – but once that's done, they're ready to cook and serve in just 5 minutes or so.

We've also included a recipe for the easiest-ever *Crispy hash browns*, which make a perfect brunch for lazy weekend mornings. If you've got friends staying over at the weekend, make the hash browns in advance and freeze them – when you're ready to eat, simply reheat them from frozen. And although our *Cheesy French bread* recipe is lovely as a snack on its own (it's the original 'tear and share' food), it's also good served alongside a bowl of soup to make it extra filling.

Spinach and ham muffin

You can't beat scrambled eggs for a quick snack, and adding spinach and ham makes this ideal for a no-fuss brunch too. You could make this with two slices of toast instead of a muffin, if you prefer.

- Serves 1 (easily multiplied)
- Ready in 10 minutes
- Not suitable for freezing

1 English muffin, split
large knob of butter
2 eggs
6 tbsp milk
handful of baby spinach leaves
1 slice ham

1 Toast the muffin, then butter it. Whisk together the eggs and milk with a pinch of salt until just combined.

2 Heat a small frying pan, then add the remaining butter and let it melt. Pour in the eggs and let them sit for 20 seconds, then stir with a wooden spoon, lifting and folding the eggs over until they are almost cooked. Add the spinach just before the eggs are ready and fold in until it wilts.

3 Top one half of the muffin with a slice of ham, pile on the scrambled eggs and then put the other muffin half on top.

Serve with tomato chutney

Eggy bread

Also known by the fancier name of French toast, this is great for a late brunch at the weekend – or any time you like, really! For a more luxurious version, you can use brioche rather than bread.

- Makes 8 triangles
- Ready in 15 minutes
- Not suitable for freezing

200ml milk
2 drops vanilla extract
¼ tsp ground cinnamon
1 egg
2 tbsp caster sugar
4 slices bread
25g butter

1 Mix the milk, vanilla extract and cinnamon in a shallow dish. Beat the egg in another dish with the sugar. Briefly dip the bread slices in the milk, then in the egg mixture to cover both sides.

2 Melt the butter in a large pan and drop the triangles. Cook for 3 minutes on each side until golden brown (you might need to do this in batches).

Serve dusted with caster sugar and drizzled with maple syrup, or with jam or fruit

Crispy hash browns

Potatoes and eggs are delicious together and these hash browns make a great change from toast at the weekend. You can make the hash browns ahead and freeze them cooked, cooled, then interleaved with foil. Unwrap them and reheat from frozen on a baking tray at fan 170C/conventional 190C/gas 5 for 15 minutes.

■ Serves 4
■ Ready in 35 minutes
■ Suitable for freezing

**650g waxy potatoes, such as
  large Charlottes
1 small onion, halved and thinly sliced
1 egg
3 tbsp sunflower oil**

1 Peel and coarsely grate the potatoes, then squeeze out as much liquid as you can with your hands – you'll be amazed at just how much will come out. Mix the potato well with seasoning and the onion and egg. Shape the mixture roughly into four to make flat, wet cakes.

2 Heat the oil in a large frying pan and fry the cakes for 5 minutes on each side until golden and cooked. You may need to use two pans or fry them in batches, if your pan isn't large enough.

Serve with poached eggs, grilled bacon and tomatoes

Cheesy French bread

This is lovely served with a bowl of soup, or just on its own as a quick snack. You can make it a day ahead and keep it in the fridge, or freeze it for up to a month. Bake it from frozen, adding 5 minutes extra to the time.

- Serves 6
- Ready in 20 minutes, plus 15 minutes in the oven
- Suitable for freezing

85g butter or garlic butter
2 tbsp chopped fresh parsley or
     spring onions
3 small baguettes
100g grated cheddar

1 Turn the oven to fan 180C/conventional 200C/gas 6. Beat the butter with the parsley or spring onions. Cut each baguette into thick slices, but don't cut all the way through as you want to keep the loaves intact. Spread the butter between each cut and add some cheese. Wrap in foil separately or in one big parcel.

2 Bake for 15 minutes until the butter and cheese have melted (big parcels will take about 5 minutes longer) and unwrap.

Salmon rarebit

This recipe gives good old cheese on toast a whole new lease of life – and canned salmon is packed with omega 3, so it's really good for you too. Horseradish gives the rarebit an extra kick, but it's not essential.

- Serves 1 (easily multiplied)
- Ready in 10 minutes
- Not suitable for freezing

1 slice granary bread
half a 212g can salmon, drained and flaked
1–2 spring onions, thinly sliced
2 tbsp cottage cheese
1 tsp grated fresh horseradish (optional)
1 tbsp grated red leicester

1 Turn the grill to high and toast the bread lightly on both sides. Mix the salmon and spring onions together and season. Spread onto the bread.

2 Mix together the cottage cheese, the horseradish (if using) and the grated cheese, then spoon on top of the salmon. Grill for 1 minute on a high shelf, then lower the shelf and continue to grill for a further 3 minutes or until the topping starts to brown.

Serve with watercress or spinach

Cheese and pepper pitta pocket

This is good as a snack or quick lunch, and a great way of using up leftover peppers in a jar. Brie is the best cheese to use, but cheddar works well too.

- Serves 1
- Ready in 5 minutes
- Not suitable for freezing

1 pitta bread
2 long slices of brie
half a roasted pepper from a jar

1 Trim off one of the long edges of the pitta bread, pop into a toaster and toast for a few seconds. Open the bread carefully to make a pocket.

2 Stuff the cheese and pepper inside the pitta and close gently. Put back into the toaster with the open side upwards and toast until the cheese has melted.

Serve with watercress or salad, if you have some

Pancake bites

These are ideal if you're going to be rushing around at the weekend as they're so quick to prepare. If you don't have basil, spread the pancakes with a little pesto.

- Makes 8
- Ready in 15 minutes
- Not suitable for freezing

1 red pepper, deseeded and sliced
140g mushrooms, finely sliced
1 tbsp olive oil
200g tub low-fat soft cheese
8 ready-made pancakes
handful of fresh basil leaves

1 Stir-fry the red pepper and mushrooms in the oil until softened.

2 Spread a little of the cheese in the centre of each pancake. Scatter over the red pepper and mushrooms. Lay three or four basil leaves on top and season.

3 Fold two opposite sides of each pancake into the centre to cover the filling then fold in the other two sides to make a square parcel. Cut in half to make two triangles.

Tomato and dolcelatte calzone

For a change from pizza, try our tasty version of this traditional Italian recipe. Dolcelatte has quite a strong taste, but you could use mozzarella if you prefer.

■ Serves 4
■ Ready in 20 minutes, plus 20 minutes rising
■ Not suitable for freezing

290g packet pizza base mix
250ml hand-hot water
2 tbsp olive oil
4 tbsp sun-dried tomato paste
6 tomatoes, roughly chopped
280g dolcelatte
175g watercress, leaves stripped from stems
1 tbsp milk

1 Make up the pizza base mix with the water and olive oil. Knead for 5 minutes.

2 Divide the dough into eight and roll four into 18cm rounds (keep the rest covered). Put each round on a piece of oiled foil on baking sheets. Spread each one with half a tbsp of tomato paste, leaving a 1cm border.

3 Divide the tomatoes among the rounds. Roughly slice the cheese and scatter on top, then top with the watercress leaves and season. Brush the edges with milk.

4 Roll the other dough pieces into four 18cm rounds. Spread with the remaining tomato paste, leaving a 1cm border. Place each one over a filled dough round, paste-side down. Press to seal the edges well. Cover each calzone loosely with oiled cling film and leave in a warm place for about 20 minutes.

5 Lightly oil a griddle pan and cook the calzone, two at a time, for 5–7 minutes on each side, until just browned and crisp (alternatively, cook under a hot grill).

Serve with a mixed green salad

Sausage and lentil pasties

These are great for feeding a crowd, or why not make a batch and freeze some of them? It's important to chill the pasties before you cook them, so that they hold their shape once they go in the oven.

- Makes 20
- Ready in 30 minutes, plus 15 minutes chilling and 15 minutes in the oven
- Suitable for freezing

1 small onion, finely chopped
1 tbsp olive oil
85g split red lentils
2 tbsp sun-dried tomato paste
300ml vegetable stock
4 sausages, skins removed
50g frozen peas
2 x 500g packs shortcrust pastry
1 egg, beaten

1 Fry the onion in the oil for 5 minutes until softened. Add the lentils and tomato paste, and cook for 2 minutes. Pour in the stock and bring to the boil. Cover and simmer for 15 minutes until most of the stock is absorbed and the lentils have softened.

2 Meanwhile, fry the sausage meat without oil for 5 minutes, breaking it up with a spoon until golden and cooked through. Add the peas and the lentils mix, season and set aside to cool.

3 Turn the oven to fan 180C/conventional 200C/gas 6. Roll out the pastry to the thickness of a £1 coin and cut out ten saucer-sized circles. Pile 3 heaped tsp of meat mixture in the middle of each circle, brush the edges with egg, fold over and press to seal. Brush with more egg, then chill for 15 minutes. Bake for 15 minutes or until golden.

Serve with coleslaw, or dunk them in soup

Beefy ciabattas

You do need to plan ahead a bit with this recipe, because the steak needs to marinate for at least a couple of hours. Get it in the fridge after breakfast and it'll be ready to cook by the time you're ready for a bite to eat.

- Makes 4 sandwiches
- Ready in 20 minutes, plus 2 hours marinating
- Not suitable for freezing

1 onion, very finely sliced
2 cloves of garlic, crushed
1 tbsp chopped fresh parsley
1 tsp dried oregano
175ml red wine
8 tbsp olive oil
1 medium rump steak, thinly sliced
2 ready-to-bake ciabatta loaves
8 radicchio leaves (red salad leaves)

1 Mix together the onion, garlic, fresh and dried herbs, wine and 6 tbsp of the olive oil. Coat the steak slices in the marinade. Cover and leave for at least 2 hours.

2 Turn the oven to fan 180C/conventional 200C/gas 6. Lift the steak slices out of the marinade and pat dry with kitchen paper. Strain the marinade and onion, reserving both. Bake the loaves according to pack instructions. Heat a frying pan to searing hot, season and fry the steak, in batches if necessary, for 2 minutes on each side. Keep warm.

3 Heat 1 tbsp of the remaining oil in the pan. Tip in the onion and fry for 2 minutes, then pour in the marinade and bubble to reduce slightly.

4 Halve the baked ciabattas lengthways. Drizzle with the remaining olive oil. Divide the lettuce between the loaves and top with the steak slices, some of the onion and juices. Cut each loaf in half and serve with wholegrain mustard.

easy
LUNCHES
recipes for a casual midday meal with friends

There's something rather decadent about sitting down to a sociable lunch on a Saturday, and every now and again it makes a change to remember it's supposed to be a day off and not just another hectic round of rushing!

So, take our advice and step out of your normal weekend routine from time to time. Invite friends and family over at midday and serve them a dish that you can prepare quickly and easily, and that everyone will relish.

The perfect casual Saturday-lunch dish is one that you can bring to the table for everyone to help themselves – which means minimum fuss for the cook. Our *Mexican fish wraps* and *Veggie chilli bean wraps* can both be assembled by your guests at the table – just put the tortillas in the middle with all the filling ingredients in little bowls.

Couscous-stuffed peppers look lovely brought to the table in the dish they were cooked in – put salad tongs or a large serving spoon out with them to make it easy for everyone to take a couple each, then all you need is a big bowl of salad to go with them. The *Red onion, mushroom and polenta tart*, and the *Tuna and corn frittata* can both come to the table with a sharp knife ready to slice them up, and putting a steaming bowl of *Crunchy cauliflower cheese* centre stage will have everyone fighting for the first spoonful.

Our *Pan-fried mozzarella parcels* look really elegant. Simply slide them from the frying pan onto the serving plates. Scatter some salad leaves around the parcels and serve, then wait for the grateful responses!

Couscous-stuffed peppers

You can roast the peppers and prepare the filling in advance, then put them in the oven when you're ready. If you want strips of roasted peppers for any other recipe, cook them as here, and when they're ready, put them in a plastic food bag for a few minutes. The steam will lift the skins so they peel off easily and you can then chop or slice the flesh.

■ Serves 4 (easily doubled or halved)
■ Ready in 15 minutes, plus 50 minutes in the oven
■ Not suitable for freezing

4 large red peppers
2 tbsp olive oil
1 onion, chopped
1 clove of garlic, chopped
1 large courgette, finely chopped
175g couscous
300ml vegetable stock
grated rind of 1 lemon
200g feta
good handful of basil, shredded
4 rounded tbsp grated parmesan

1 Turn the oven to fan 180C/conventional 200C/gas 6. Halve the peppers through the stalks, then remove the seeds and membrane, but leave the stalks. Arrange the peppers in a roasting tin, drizzle with 1 tbsp of the oil and season. Bake for 30 minutes until almost tender.

2 Fry the onion in the remaining oil until soft and lightly browned. Add the garlic and courgette and cook gently for 5 minutes. Remove from the heat and stir in the couscous and stock. Cover and leave for 5 minutes until the couscous has absorbed the liquid.

3 Cool slightly, then stir in the lemon rind, feta, basil and some seasoning. Spoon into the roasted peppers and sprinkle with the parmesan. Bake for 20 minutes or until the cheese is lightly browned.

Serve with a green salad and crusty bread

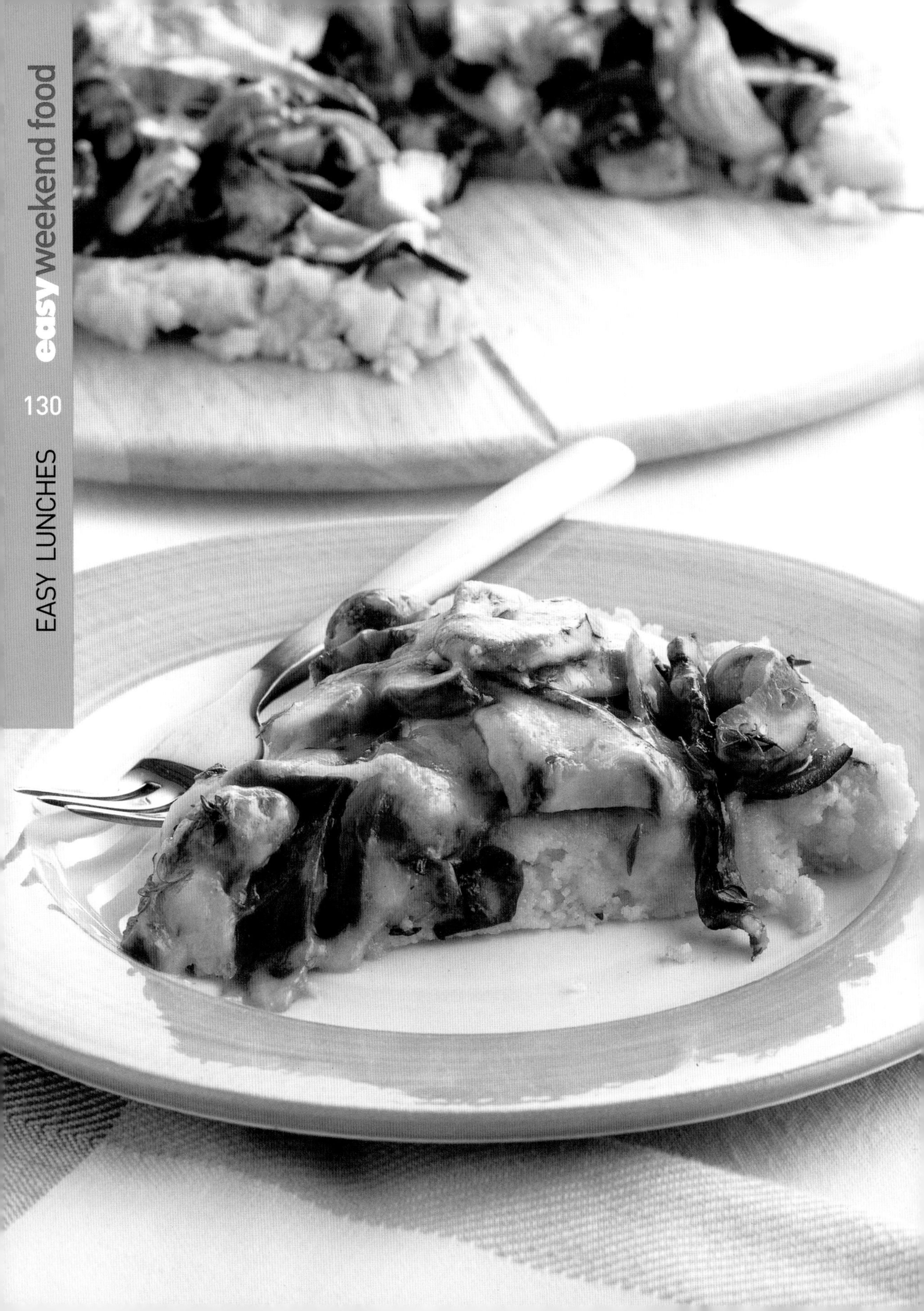

Red onion, mushroom and polenta tart

A polenta base makes a change from pastry and is really easy to make. You can also serve the flavoured polenta in place of mashed potato – follow the instructions in step 1, taking it from the heat as soon as it's thickened, and serve it immediately, before it has a chance to start setting.

- Serves 2–3
- Ready in 35 minutes
- Not suitable for freezing

140g instant polenta
50g grated parmesan
4 sun-dried tomatoes in oil, drained and chopped
2 tsp fresh thyme leaves
2 cloves of garlic, thinly sliced
1 red onion, cut into thin wedges
4 tbsp olive oil
170g chestnut mushrooms, some halved, some sliced
85g grated cheddar

1 Turn on the grill to high and lightly oil a large baking tray. Pour 600ml of water into a large saucepan and bring to the boil. Pour in the polenta, stirring all the time, then bring back to the boil. Lower the heat and simmer, stirring, for 5 minutes until very thick. Remove from the heat and stir in the parmesan, sun-dried tomatoes and half of the thyme. Tip the mixture onto the baking tray and spread into a rough round shape, about 23cm across.

2 Grill the polenta base for about 10 minutes until it is set and just beginning to brown. Meanwhile, fry the garlic and onion in the oil until they begin to soften and turn golden. Toss in the mushrooms and cook for 3 minutes. Remove the polenta base from the grill.

3 Spread the mushroom mixture over the base, sprinkle over the cheddar and the remaining thyme, and grill until the cheese has melted.

Mexican fish wraps

Spray oil is very useful when you're grilling fish – you can avoid using more than you really need, and you can coat the fish evenly without damaging the delicate flesh.

- ■ Serves 4
- ■ Ready in 15 minutes
- ■ Not suitable for freezing

**finely grated rind and juice of 1 lime
700g skinless white fish fillet, like cod or
    haddock, cut into thick strips
2 egg whites, beaten
100g fresh breadcrumbs
4 squirts of oil spray
200g pot tzatziki
8 small, soft flour tortilla wraps
small wedge iceberg lettuce, shredded**

1 Turn on the grill to medium. Sprinkle the lime rind over the fish, then season. Dip the fish into the egg whites, then coat with breadcrumbs and place on a baking sheet. Spray the fish with 2 squirts of oil, then grill for 2 minutes. Turn them over, spray with more oil, then grill for a further 2 minutes until the fish is cooked and the breadcrumbs are golden.

2 Squeeze the lime juice into the tzatziki and stir. Warm the tortillas according to pack instructions. To assemble the wraps, place a handful of lettuce onto the top two-thirds of a tortilla, then rest 3 fish fingers on top with a good spoonful of lime tzatziki. Fold to make a wrap.

Veggie chilli bean wraps

These are ideal for eating with your hands, but do make sure you've got some napkins or paper towels as they can be quite messy! You can make mini versions of these to serve at a party too – cut each filled, rolled wrap into two with a sharp knife and arrange on a tray.

- ■ Serves 4
- ■ Ready in 20 minutes
- ■ Suitable for freezing

**1 small onion, sliced
1 tbsp sunflower oil
400g can mixed beans, drained and rinsed
400g can chopped tomatoes
30g sachet fajita seasoning
8 soft corn tortilla wraps
100g grated cheddar
170g tub guacamole
142ml tub soured cream
handful of fresh parsley or coriander
    (optional)**

1 Fry the onion in the oil for 5 minutes until soft. Tip in the beans, tomatoes and spicy seasoning. Simmer for 10 minutes, stirring occasionally.

2 Warm the wraps under the grill or in the microwave for 1 minute. Spoon a large spoonful of beans into the centre of each wrap, top with some grated cheese and a spoonful each of guacamole and soured cream. Sprinkle over some fresh herbs, if you like, then roll up.

Perfect jacket potatoes

Jackets potatoes are the ultimate easy dish, especially if you cook them in the microwave for speed, and there's no end to the delicious things you can fill them with. For a crispy skin, follow the microwave instructions in step 1, reducing the cooking time to 7 minutes, then put the potatoes in a really hot oven for 15 minutes.

- Serves 2
- Ready in 10 minutes
- Not suitable for freezing

1 Wash and dry 2 large potatoes and prick them all over with a fork (Maris Piper is the best variety for baking). Sit each on a piece of kitchen paper in the microwave, then cook on High for 8 minutes or until they are softened. Leave to stand for 1 minute. If you cook more than 2 potatoes at a time, you may need to increase the cooking time slightly.

2 Cut a cross in the top of each jacket potato and squeeze the base to open them. Fill with your chosen topping, or try one of the following ideas:

Salami and red pepper pesto filling

- Serves 2
- Ready in 10 minutes
- Not suitable for freezing

2 rounded tbsp crème fraîche
1 rounded tsp pesto
2 red peppers from a jar, sliced
6 salami slices, sliced
6 pitted black olives, halved

Mix the crème fraîche and pesto. Pile the peppers and salami into the hot potatoes, top with the olives, then spoon the crème-fraîche mix on top.

Spicy bacon and mushroom filling

- Serves 2
- Ready in 10 minutes
- Not suitable for freezing

100g streaky bacon, chopped
knob of butter
100g chestnut mushrooms, sliced
150g tub fresh tomato salsa

Fry the bacon without any oil until crisp. Add the butter to the pan then add the mushrooms and fry for about 5 minutes until brown. Season. Spoon plenty of tomato salsa into the potatoes, then top with the bacon and mushrooms and a little more salsa.

Stilton and watercress filling

- Serves 2
- Ready in 10 minutes
- Not suitable for freezing

85g stilton
2 handfuls of watercress
2 tbsp mango chutney

Mash half the stilton with a fork and chop the watercress. Spoon the mashed stilton into the two hot potatoes with half the mango chutney. Place the watercress inside, then crumble over the remaining cheese and top with the rest of the chutney.

Red pepper and parmesan pizzas

This must be the easiest recipe for a homemade pizza base dough! The topping is vegetarian, but if you are serving it to meat-eaters you could also add slices of ham or pepperoni, or flaked tuna.

- Serves 4
- Ready in 20 minutes
- Not suitable for freezing

50g parmesan
225g self-raising flour
50g butter
125ml milk
4–6 tbsp pesto
2 large roasted peppers from a jar
12 olives
good handful of rocket

1 Turn the oven to fan 200C/conventional 220C/gas 7 and grease two baking trays. Finely grate half the parmesan in a food processor. Add the flour, butter and a good pinch of salt, then whizz until all of the butter has been incorporated. Add the milk, then mix to a soft, slightly sticky dough.

2 Flour your fingers and divide the dough into four, then press each piece into a rough circle about the size of a saucer. Thickly spread with the pesto, then tear each pepper into six pieces and arrange on top with the olives. Bake for 10 minutes until golden. Top with rocket and shave over the remaining cheese.

Serve with green salad

Lemon tuna mayo pasta

Most of the ingredients for this recipe are the kind of things you'll have to hand already, except perhaps the dill – you can use fresh parsley instead, if you like.

- Serves 4
- Ready in 15 minutes
- Not suitable for freezing

225g tagliatelle
175g mayonnaise
125ml milk
1 tsp frozen or freeze-dried dill
2 x 185g cans tuna chunks in brine, drained and flaked
3 tbsp capers, drained (optional)
grated rind of 1 lemon, plus a squeeze of juice

1 Cook the pasta according to pack instructions, then drain.

2 Meanwhile, beat together the mayonnaise, milk and dill, then stir in the tuna, capers, if using, and lemon rind. Add a squeeze of juice and season.

3 Mix the tuna with the pasta and toss well, then pile into bowls to serve.

Pan-fried mozzarella parcels

This is ideal for a lovely, light weekend lunch with friends, served with plenty of crusty bread. The sharp balsamic dressing makes a good contrast to the melting mozzarella and you could add some green olives to the lettuce and avocado too, if you like.

- Serves 4
- Ready in 15 minutes
- Not suitable for freezing

4 x 100g balls mozzarella, drained
12 slices prosciutto
2 tbsp olive oil
½ frisée lettuce, washed and torn
2 ripe avocados, peeled, stoned and sliced
1 tbsp balsamic vinegar

1 Chop each mozzarella ball into three and wrap each piece in a slice of prosciutto. Heat the oil in a pan until very hot. Season the parcels with pepper, then fry for a few minutes on each side until the ham is brown and crisp and the mozzarella melting.

2 Divide the lettuce among four plates and scatter over the avocado slices. Remove the mozzarella parcels from the pan and arrange three on each plate.

3 Pour the balsamic vinegar into the pan and stir to combine with the cooking juices. Drizzle over the leaves and parcels.

Serve with chutney and ciabatta bread

Tuna and corn frittata

A frittata is a more substantial version of an omelette, with sliced potatoes as well as eggs. New potatoes work best for this because they fry well and won't break up.

- Serves 4
- Ready in 35 minutes
- Not suitable for freezing

1 tbsp olive oil
175g new potatoes, cut into chunks
3 spring onions, chopped
½ red pepper, deseeded and sliced
198g can sweetcorn, drained
100g can tuna in brine, drained
4 large eggs, beaten with seasoning

1 Cook the potatoes in the oil in a non-stick frying pan for about 12 minutes, stirring until golden. Add the onion and pepper, and cook for a few minutes more.

2 Stir in the sweetcorn and tuna then pour the eggs over the mixture and cook gently for 5–8 minutes until the eggs start to set. Grill to brown and set the top.

Serve with salad and ketchup

Crunchy cauliflower cheese

Scattering toasted hazelnuts over the top of this takes it to a whole new level, and using a tub of ready-made cheese sauce means it can be ready in minutes. Add a couple of rashers of bacon on the side, if you like.

■ Serves 4
■ Ready in 15 minutes
■ Not suitable for freezing

1 large cauliflower, broken into florets
350g tub fresh cheese sauce
100g cheddar, grated
25g toasted hazelnuts, crushed (optional)
50g fresh breadcrumbs

1 Turn on the grill to high. Fill a large saucepan with water and bring to the boil. Cook the cauliflower for 7 minutes until tender.

2 Heat the sauce either in the microwave on High for 1 minute or in a small pan until warmed through, but not boiling. Put the cheese, nuts, if using, and the breadcrumbs into a bowl and mix together.

3 Drain the cauliflower and place in the bottom of a large, shallow baking dish. Pour over the warmed sauce, covering evenly, then sprinkle with the breadcrumbs. Put under the grill for 5 minutes, or until the cheese is bubbling and the breadcrumbs are golden.

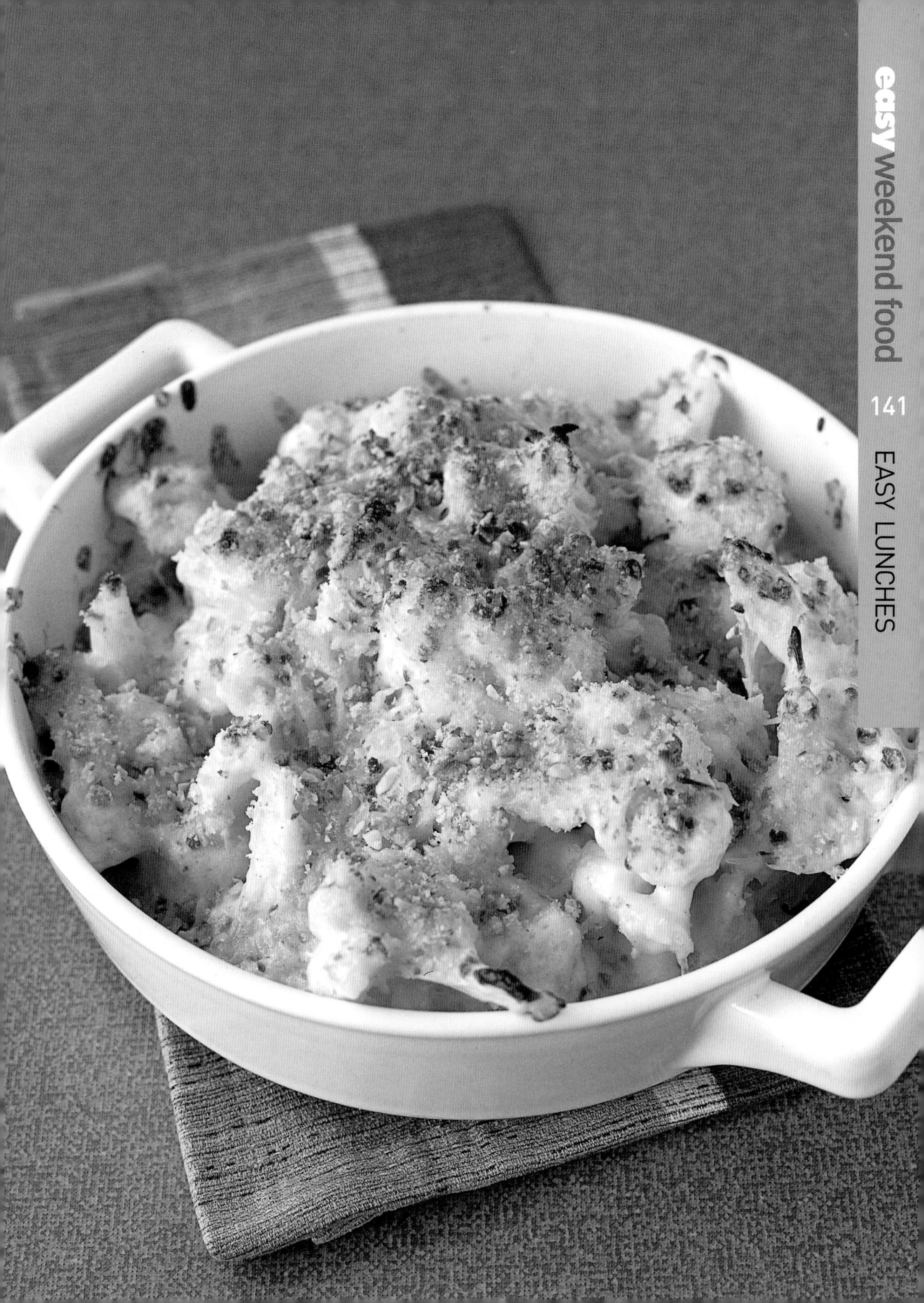

easy
ENTERTAINING
fuss-free recipes for meals you can linger over

For anyone new to cooking, entertaining can be a daunting experience. And more experienced cooks can get tired of being tied to the kitchen and missing out on the conversation while their guests are arriving and relaxing with a glass of wine.

Having too many things to do at the last minute is a common mistake – and it can turn an otherwise enjoyable experience into a trauma. Inviting friends over for a meal doesn't have to be stressful (or time-consuming), though. And if you plan your meal carefully, you can get much of it done before everyone arrives so there are only a few things left to finish off at the end.

Try to make sure at least one course can be completely ready well ahead of time, so all you need to do on the night is bring it to the table. The starters in this 'Easy Entertaining' chapter can all be prepared in advance, and the only one that needs any last-minute

attention is the *Spiced root soup with crisp onions* – it just has to be quickly reheated and the onion garnish fried, ready to sprinkle over.

From our selection of main courses, the *Salmon and watercress parcels* and *Steak and wild mushroom pies* can both be partially prepared ahead, and the *Chicken with 40 cloves of garlic* and *Quick roast pork* are quick and easy to prep and can then be left to cook happily in the oven.

Finally, all our desserts can be made in advance – the *Poached plum crème brûlée* just needs to be popped under the grill before you serve it.

Have fun creating your own menus by mixing and matching our starters, mains and desserts. To get you started, here are some of our favourite combinations:

MENU 1 – Casual dinner party

- **Starter** Mozzarella with tomato and chilli salsa
- **Main course** Tarragon chicken in a bag
- **Dessert** Mango and lime trifle

MENU 2 – Posh dinner party

- **Starter** Herby crab and avocado tarts
- **Main course** Chicken with 40 cloves of garlic
- **Dessert** Poached plum crème brûlée

MENU 3 – Sunday lunch

- **Starter** Chicken liver pâté
- **Main course** Quick roast pork
- **Dessert** Summer berry slices

Mozzarella with tomato and chilli salsa

This is a wonderful starter for a warm, sunny day, especially if you're dining out of doors. To add to the relaxed feel, serve it on a wooden board and let everyone help themselves.

▪ Serves 6
▪ Ready in 10 minutes
▪ Not suitable for freezing

2 x 100g packs mozzarella, drained
5 plum tomatoes, roughly chopped
1 red chilli, deseeded and finely chopped
1 small red onion, chopped
1 tbsp sun-dried tomato paste
2 tbsp fresh flat-leaf parsley, chopped
1 tbsp lemon juice
3 tbsp olive oil, plus extra for drizzling

1 Slice the mozzarella and arrange in a slightly overlapping circle on a board or serving platter.

2 Put the remaining ingredients in a mixing bowl, add seasoning and mix together. Just before serving, spoon the salsa over the mozzarella and drizzle with a little olive oil.

Serve with crusty bread

Chicken liver pâté

Chicken livers are really good value, so this is an excellent starter if you're entertaining on a budget. If you have a bottle of sherry in the cupboard, add a tablespoon at the end of step 1 to give the pâté an extra zing. You can make it in advance and keep it in the fridge for up to 2 days.

▪ Serves 4
▪ Ready in 15 minutes, plus chilling time
▪ Suitable for freezing

25g butter
400g chicken livers
3 cloves of garlic, roughly chopped
2 tsp light muscovado sugar

1 Melt the butter and cook the livers and garlic for 5 minutes, until the livers are browned on the outside and still a little pink inside. Stir in the sugar, season well and allow to cool for 5 minutes.

2 Whizz the chicken livers and buttery juices to a paste in a food processor until completely smooth. Pour into a bowl, cover with cling film and chill for an hour or overnight.

Serve with toast triangles or crackers, plus a few salad leaves, if you like

Warm stuffed avocados

Baked avocados were on every trendy restaurant menu in the Seventies – and we think it's time they came back into fashion again! We've given them a 21st-century twist by grilling them (much quicker than cooking them in the oven) and stuffing them with sun-dried tomatoes and olives.

■ Serves 4
■ Ready in 15 minutes
■ Not suitable for freezing

2 large ripe avocados
3 tbsp olive oil
1 plum tomato, deseeded and chopped
4 sun-dried tomatoes in oil, drained and chopped
50g pitted black olives, quartered
2 spring onions, finely sliced on the diagonal
1 tbsp capers
1 tbsp each freshly squeezed orange, lemon and lime juice
1 tbsp cider vinegar
2 tsp caster sugar
2 large fresh torn basil leaves

1 Turn on the grill to high. Halve the avocados and discard the stones. Brush each half with ½ tsp of the olive oil and arrange on a baking sheet. Grill for 5 minutes.

2 In a small bowl, toss together all the remaining ingredients. Season, then pile on top of the avocados. Serve immediately.

Spiced root soup with crisp onions

The crisp onion garnish is easy to make, but it transforms this soup from an ordinary dish into something that looks really special. Its taste and rich texture make it ideal for winter entertaining.

■ Serves 4
■ Ready in 1 hour
■ Not suitable for freezing

2 onions, thinly sliced
3 tbsp vegetable oil
1 tsp mustard seeds
1 tsp cumin seeds
2 leeks, sliced
3 carrots, sliced
2 medium potatoes, chopped
2 parsnips, chopped
2–3 tsp curry paste
1.2 litres vegetable stock
250ml natural yogurt
handful of fresh coriander, chopped

1 Fry half the onions in 2 tbsp of the oil for 3 minutes. Add the mustard and cumin seeds, and fry until browned.

2 Add the vegetables and curry paste, and stir until well coated. Pour in the stock and bring to the boil. Reduce the heat, partly cover and simmer for 30 minutes, until the vegetables are tender. Meanwhile, heat the remaining oil in a small pan, add the remaining onion and fry quickly until browned. Drain on kitchen paper.

3 Purée the soup in a blender in batches, then return to the pan and stir in most of the yogurt. Season. Reheat gently, then ladle into bowls and top each with a spoonful of the remaining yogurt, some fried onions and some chopped coriander.

Herby crab and avocado tarts

These look very fancy, but they're not difficult to make. The crab is covered in a delicate, delicious hollandaise sauce and this is the easiest-ever recipe for making it. You can also use the sauce to pour over lightly cooked asparagus when it's in season in the summer. The tart cases can be made up to 3 days ahead and stored in an airtight tin, and the sauce can be prepared up to the end of step 2, then kept covered in the fridge for up to 3 days.

- Serves 8
- Ready in 45 minutes
- Not suitable for freezing

8 medium slices white bread
50g butter, melted
4 tbsp white wine vinegar
½ tsp peppercorns
1 fresh bay leaf
2 ripe avocados, halved, stoned and peeled
juice of 1 lemon
100g bag wild rocket
400g white crabmeat (fresh or canned)
4 egg yolks
250g pack unsalted butter
small handful of fresh chervil or tarragon,
**   roughly chopped**

1 Turn the oven to fan 180C/conventional 200C/gas 6. Cut a circle from the centre of each slice of bread using a 10cm round cutter and roll flat with a rolling pin. Brush the circles with the melted butter on each side, then press into eight individual tart tins. Lift the tart tins onto two baking sheets and bake for 10 minutes or until tinged golden at the edges. Carefully flip the cases out of the tins so they are upside down on the sheets, then put back into the oven for 5 minutes, or until crisp and dry. Leave to cool.

2 Put the vinegar, peppercorns and bay leaf into a small pan, and bring to the boil. Simmer for about 5 minutes, or until reduced to about 1 tbsp. Take off the heat, then strain out the bay leaf and peppercorns.

3 Thinly slice the avocados, put into a bowl and gently toss with a little of the lemon juice (this can be kept covered in the fridge for up to 2 hours before serving).

4 When ready to serve, put the avocado and a little rocket into each case, then top with crabmeat. Tip the cooled vinegar mixture into a tall, narrow jug, then add the egg yolks. Melt the butter in a pan over a medium heat (don't boil), then add to the jug. Put a stick blender right to the bottom of the jug, turn on and draw very slowly up through the butter. The sauce will thicken as the yolks and butter meld together. Add the herbs, season, then add a dash of the remaining lemon juice. Spoon the hollandaise generously over each tartlet, so it oozes over the crab. Serve immediately.

Salmon and watercress parcels

For a substantial main course, serve this with new potatoes and green beans. But if you want everyone to have enough room for dessert, it's just as good with a simple green salad.

◼ Serves 4
◼ Ready in 15 minutes, plus 20 minutes in the oven
◼ Not suitable for freezing

80g watercress
50g soft butter
500g shortcrust pastry
4 skinless salmon fillets
1 egg, beaten

1 Turn the oven to fan 170C/conventional 190C/gas 5. Whizz the watercress and butter in a food processor to make a paste, then season.

2 Roll out the pastry on a lightly floured surface to ½cm thickness and divide into four squares. Put a salmon fillet onto each square and cover with a layer of the watercress paste. Brush the edges of the pastry with egg, then fold over and join them together so the salmon is completely covered. Trim off any excess pastry so you have a neat parcel shape. Brush the top with more egg and bake for 20 minutes until golden brown and crisp.

Quick roast pork

Pork loin cooks quickly in the oven so it's a good cut to use for a speedy Sunday roast. It's quite lean, so wrapping it in bacon prevents it from drying out.

◼ Serves 4
◼ Ready in 20 minutes, plus 30 minutes in the oven
◼ Not suitable for freezing

2 pork loins
½ tsp dried thyme
8 rashers rindless streaky bacon
2 tbsp olive oil
750g potatoes, thinly sliced
1 onion, chopped
250g mushrooms, quartered
2 tbsp sherry
1 tbsp grainy mustard
200ml tub crème fraîche

1 Turn the oven to fan 170C/conventional 190C/gas 5. Season the pork and sprinkle over the thyme. Stretch the bacon with the back of a knife, then wrap four rashers around each loin.

2 Fry the pork in the oil over a high heat until lightly browned. Put in a roasting tin. Fry the potatoes until just starting to colour, then season. Arrange around the pork and roast for 30 minutes until the potatoes are crisp and golden.

3 Meanwhile, fry the onion in the pan you used for the pork, until soft. Add the mushrooms and fry over a high heat for 3 minutes. Stir in the sherry, mustard and crème fraîche. Season. Cook until tender. Slice the pork and arrange over the mushrooms, with the potatoes.

Serve with broccoli and spring greens

Chicken with 40 cloves of garlic

Forty cloves might sound a lot, but once roasted with butter and a little sugar they add a delicious, soft flavour to the sauce. Use half butter and half oil to fry the chicken – the butter adds flavour and the oil stops it burning.

- Serves 4
- Ready in 30 minutes, plus 1 hour in the oven
- Not suitable for freezing

3 garlic heads (about 40 cloves)
25g butter, plus a little extra
1 tsp caster sugar
4 boneless chicken breasts, skin on
1 tbsp olive oil
1 onion, finely chopped
100ml chicken stock
100ml white wine
2 fresh thyme sprigs or a pinch of dried thyme
1 tbsp plain flour
handful of chopped fresh parsley

1 Turn the oven to fan 150C/conventional 170C/gas 3. Cook the garlic in boiling water for 3 minutes. Peel the cloves, reserve one and bake the rest in an ovenproof dish with the knob of butter and the sugar for an hour, shaking occasionally.

2 Meanwhile, fry the chicken, skin-side down, in the butter and oil for 7 minutes, turning until browned. Remove to a plate. Fry the onion for 5 minutes, add the chicken with the stock, wine, thyme and reserved garlic clove, chopped. Bring to a simmer then cook in the oven for 35 minutes.

3 Take the chicken from the pan and keep warm. Boil the pan juices for 5 minutes. Remove the whole garlic cloves from their dish, stir the flour into their juices to make a paste, then add to the chicken juices, stirring until smooth and thickened. Add the garlic cloves, coat the chicken with the sauce and sprinkle with the parsley.

Serve with potatoes and green beans

Quick tomato risotto

Using the microwave to make this risotto speeds things up considerably. If you're cooking and eating in the same room, you can carry on chatting to your guests while you're making it.

- Serves 4
- Ready in 20 minutes
- Not suitable for freezing

250g risotto rice
1 onion, finely chopped
50g butter
250ml vegetable stock
500ml jar of passata
500g punnet cherry tomatoes
100g ball mozzarella, drained and cut into large chunks

1 Tip the rice, onion and half the butter into a large microwaveable bowl. Cover and cook in the microwave on High for 3 minutes. Stir in the stock and passata, then continue to cook, uncovered, for 10 minutes. Give it a good stir and mix in the tomatoes and mozzarella. Microwave on High for another 8 minutes until the rice is cooked and the tomatoes are soft.

2 Leave the risotto to cool for a few minutes, then stir in the remaining butter.

Serve sprinkled with grated parmesan and shredded fresh basil

Polenta with mushrooms and sage butter

Polenta works best with strong flavours and adding fresh sage to this buttery mushroom topping really makes the most of it. Season the polenta at the end of step 1, then taste it and add a little more cheese if necessary.

- Serves 2
- Ready in 20 minutes
- Not suitable for freezing

100g instant polenta
25g grated parmesan
100g butter
2 handfuls mixed mushrooms, halved, quartered or sliced
a few fresh sage leaves, shredded

1 Make up the polenta according to pack instructions, then beat in the cheese with half the butter and season well. It will become quite soft and creamy.

2 Melt the remaining butter in a pan and cook the mushrooms until golden. Add the sage and stir. Serve the polenta topped with the mushroom mix, and some extra parmesan shavings, if you like.

Steak and wild mushroom pies

You can use chestnut or button mushrooms for this recipe, if you prefer, but wild mushrooms (usually available in supermarkets in the autumn) give the pies a special flavour.

- Serves 6
- Ready in 40 minutes
- Suitable for freezing (filling only)

375g pack ready-rolled puff pastry
1 egg, beaten
2 tbsp olive oil
1 large onion, chopped
250g mixed wild mushrooms, thickly sliced
700g sirloin steak, trimmed of any fat and
    cut into thin strips
850ml beef stock
150ml red wine
4 tbsp caramelized red onions, from a jar
1 heaped tsp Dijon mustard
2 tbsp fresh parsley, chopped

1 Turn the oven to fan 180C/conventional 200C/gas 6. Cut out six rounds of puff pastry. Put them on a baking sheet and mark a fine lattice on the top of each with the tip of a sharp knife. Brush with the beaten egg and bake in the oven for 10 minutes, or until golden and puffed.

2 While the pastry is cooking, heat 1 tbsp of the oil in a frying pan. Fry the onion until softened, then add the mushrooms and cook for 2 minutes. Season with freshly ground black pepper and transfer to a plate. Heat the remaining oil and add half the steak. Season and fry for 3 minutes, turning frequently, then transfer to a plate. Repeat with the remaining meat, then remove.

3 Pour the beef stock, red wine and caramelized onions into the pan, stir in the mushroom and onion mixture, and simmer for 5 minutes. Tip in the meat and cook for 1 minute. Stir the mustard and parsley into the sauce, divide the steak and mushroom mixture among six plates and top each serving with a pastry lid.

Serve with seasonal veg

Tarragon chicken in a bag

Cooking the chicken in a paper parcel keeps it moist. Bring the parcels to the table and let each guest open their own so they can enjoy the delicious aromas as they peel back the paper.

■ Serves 4
■ Ready in 50 minutes
■ Not suitable for freezing

1 tbsp olive oil
25g butter
4 boneless, skinless chicken breasts
175g baby carrots, whole or halved lengthways
3 baby turnips, peeled and thinly sliced
4 shallots, quartered
300ml white wine
450g frozen broad beans
15g pack fresh tarragon, chopped

1 Turn the oven to fan 170C/conventional 190C/gas 5. Heat the oil and half the butter in a frying pan. Fry the chicken for 4 minutes over a high heat to brown, remove and set aside. Fry the carrots, turnips and shallots for 4 minutes, then remove with a slotted spoon. Swirl the wine into the pan, scraping up any crispy bits, and bubble until it has reduced to about 5 tbsp. Remove from the heat and then stir in the remaining butter.

2 Cut four 35cm-diameter circles from baking parchment or greaseproof paper. Divide the prepared veg and the broad beans among the circles and top with the chicken breasts and the wine-butter reduction. Scatter over the tarragon and season. Fold the paper over to enclose, then twist the edges to seal. Put on a baking sheet and bake for 20–25 minutes. Serve in the parcels for your guests to unwrap.

Serve with potatoes and a spoonful of crème fraîche

Spicy lamb with warm couscous

You'll find harissa paste with the herbs and spices in the supermarket. It's an easy way to add extra heat to this dish and it goes really well with couscous, which is always best served with strong flavours to give it a boost.

- Serves 4
- Ready in 15 minutes
- Not suitable for freezing

250g couscous
400g can chickpeas, drained and rinsed
grated rind of 1 lemon
350ml hot chicken stock
3 tsp harissa paste
4 lamb chops
150g tub natural yogurt
handful of rocket, to garnish

1 Turn on the grill to medium. Tip the couscous, chickpeas and lemon rind into a large bowl, and pour over the hot stock. Cover with cling film and leave to stand for 10 minutes, until all the stock has been absorbed.

2 Meanwhile, smear 2 tsp of the harissa paste over the chops, season, then grill for 4 minutes on each side until crisp on the outside and medium rare in the middle. Cover, then rest for a few minutes. Mix the remaining harissa into the yogurt. Season.

3 Break up any clumps in the couscous with a fork and scatter the rocket over just before serving with the chops.

Serve with a spoonful of the harissa dressing on each plate

Oriental salmon

To make the garnish, snip the green parts of each spring onion just above its white bulb to give you 5cm lengths, then cut each strip in half lengthways and scatter over the cooked fish.

- Serves 4
- Ready in 15 minutes
- Not suitable for freezing

1 tbsp clear honey
1 tbsp wholegrain mustard
2 tbsp soy sauce
grated rind and juice of 1 lime
4 skinless salmon fillets
2 spring onions, shredded

1 Mix the honey with the mustard, soy sauce, lime rind and juice and 3 tbsp of water.

2 Cook the salmon in a large, non-stick frying pan for 5 minutes (there's no need to add oil). Flip the salmon over, then pour over the soy mixture and bring to the boil. Sprinkle over the spring onions and bubble for 1–2 minutes, until heated through.

Serve with stir-fried vegetables and rice

Cappuccino cups

You can make these up to a day ahead and keep them, covered with cling film, in the fridge. If you don't have suitable cups, you can make this in one large dish instead.

- Makes 6
- Ready in 20 minutes
- Not suitable for freezing

350g pack Madeira cake, thinly sliced
300ml strong black coffee
3 tbsp Tia Maria (optional)
3 tbsp caster sugar
100g dark chocolate, grated
50g toasted flaked almonds
568ml carton whipping cream

1 Put half the cake slices in the base of six teacups. Mix the coffee, Tia Maria (if using) and 1 tbsp of the sugar, then drizzle half over the cake. Sprinkle with a third of the grated chocolate and half the flaked almonds, then repeat the layers of sponge, coffee, chocolate and almonds – reserving the final third of chocolate.

2 Whip the cream with the remaining sugar until it holds its shape. Spoon into the cups and sprinkle with the rest of the chocolate. Chill until ready to serve.

Mango and lime trifle

This brings good old-fashioned trifle up to date. You can use orange juice instead of Cointreau to soak the sponge fingers, if you prefer. But don't be tempted to use lemon instead of lime juice – mango and lime are the perfect match.

- Serves 6
- Ready in 10 minutes
- Not suitable for freezing

8 trifle sponges
3 tbsp marmalade
425g can mango slices, drained and juice reserved
grated rind and juice of 1 lime
4 tbsp Cointreau
425g can custard
284ml carton whipping cream
2 tbsp icing sugar
2 chocolate flakes, crumbled

1 Slice the trifle sponges in half (so they are thinner), spread with marmalade and sandwich together again. Put 4 sponges in the base of a large glass bowl. Chop the mango, then scatter over the sponges.

2 Mix the mango juice with the lime juice and Cointreau, and pour half of it over the sponges. Arrange the remaining sponges on top then pour over the rest of the juice mixture. Leave for a few minutes, then gently squash down with the back of a spoon.

3 Pour the custard over the sponges. Lightly whip the cream and sugar with the lime rind – it should be spoonable and softly holding its shape. Spoon over the custard and chill for a couple of hours, or overnight if more convenient. Serve scattered with the chocolate flakes.

Cheat's blackberry meringue cake

Lining the tin with cling film is a good idea when you're making frozen desserts like this as it makes them so easy to lift out. Soften this for an hour in the fridge to make it easier to cut.

- Serves 8
- Ready in 10 minutes, plus 6 hours freezing time
- Suitable for freezing

568ml carton double cream
85g caster sugar
4 meringue nests
450g blackberries, plus 225g to serve
icing sugar, for dusting

1 Line a 23cm-round loose-based cake tin with cling film. Whip the cream until it just holds its shape, then stir in the sugar. Break the meringue nests into small pieces and lightly mash the blackberries with a fork. Stir the meringues and the blackberries lightly into the cream.

2 Spoon the dessert mixture into the tin, then smooth the top. Cover and freeze until firm – about 6 hours. It will keep in the freezer for up to a month.

3 To serve, turn out onto a serving plate and peel off the cling film. Scatter over the extra berries and sift with icing sugar.

Chilled lemon cheesecake

This has to be the simplest lemon cheesecake ever – it magically sets on its own in the fridge so you don't need to use gelatine, which can be a bit fiddly.

- Serves 8
- Ready in 20 minutes, plus chilling
- Not suitable for freezing

85g digestive biscuits
40g butter
200g pack soft cheese
397g can condensed milk
finely grated rind and juice of 2 lemons
142ml carton double cream

1 Put the biscuits in a plastic food bag and crush to crumbs with a rolling pin or the base of a pan. Melt the butter in a large pan, add the biscuit crumbs. Mix well. Tip into a 20cm-deep, loose-bottomed cake tin and press down firmly and evenly with the back of a spoon to make a thin layer. Chill while you make the filling.

2 Beat the cheese and condensed milk until smooth (preferably with an electric whisk), then add the lemon rind and juice. When mixed, beat in the cream. Pour onto the biscuit base, smooth the top and chill overnight (or for at least 5 hours) until set.

3 To serve, loosen the edges of the cheesecake with a knife, press up the base and lift the cheesecake onto a serving plate. Leave plain, or decorate with lemon slices and dust with icing sugar.

Poached plum crème brûlée

The great thing about plums is that you can poach them when they're not really ripe enough to eat, and they become wonderfully sweet and juicy in the sugary syrup.

■ Serves 6
■ Ready in 20 minutes, plus 4 hours chilling
■ Not suitable for freezing

200g caster sugar, plus 2 tbsp extra
1 cinnamon stick
1 vanilla pod, split and seeds scraped from the middle
500g plums, quartered and stones removed
250g tub mascarpone

1 Tip the 200g of the sugar into a pan with 225ml of water, the cinnamon stick and vanilla seeds. Gently heat until the sugar dissolves. Slide the fruit into the syrup. Bring the mixture to the boil, then let it simmer for about 5 minutes or until the plums are soft (the time will vary, depending on the ripeness of the plums).

2 Strain the plums and pour all the liquid back into the pan. Reduce the liquid by half until very sweet and sticky. Fill six ramekins two-thirds full with plums and add 1 tbsp of the syrup to each. Wait for this to cool, then divide the mascarpone among the ramekins. Smooth the surface with a knife and refrigerate for 4 hours. Turn on the grill to high, sprinkle over the remaining sugar and place under the grill until it caramelizes. Leave the caramel to harden for a minute, then serve.

Summer berry slices

Another twist on a classic, this quirky version of a summer pudding uses slices of Madeira cake instead of bread. If you're serving it to adults, you could use crème de cassis (blackcurrant liqueur) in place of the cordial.

■ Serves 6
■ Ready in 35 minutes, plus overnight chilling
■ Not suitable for freezing

1kg mixed berries (such as strawberries, blackcurrants, blueberries, redcurrants and raspberries)
100g caster sugar
2 tbsp blackcurrant cordial (optional)
450g plain Madeira cake, sliced lengthways into 3 long strips

1 Line the base of a 1kg loaf tin with a long strip of double-thickness baking parchment, allowing it to overhang at the narrow ends. Remove the stalks from the strawberries and halve or slice them if large. Put the currants into a pan with the sugar and 3 tbsp of water and bring to the boil, stirring. Simmer for 5 minutes until softened, add the remaining fruits and cook for 2 minutes more. Remove from the heat, add the cordial, if using, then cool.

2 Cover the base of the tin with a layer of cake and trim to fit. Spoon in half the fruits, with a little juice. Fit another layer of cake on top, spoon over the remaining fruits and finally top with the last slice of cake. Keep the leftover juice. Press lightly to squash the fruits into the cake, cover with clingfilm and put a can of beans on top to weigh it down. Chill overnight.

3 Using the overhanging paper, lift the cake out of the tin and onto a plate. Spoon over enough of the leftover juice to moisten.

Serve with shop-bought fruit coulis and cream or mascarpone

easy
BAKING
delicious ideas for afternoon tea – or to enjoy in your coffee break

If there's one kind of cooking that most people enjoy more than any other, it's baking. For many of us, our earliest memories are of helping our mum or our granny to bake, and there's something immensely comforting and timeless about the delicious aromas that waft from the oven when there are biscuits or cakes on the go.

Sadly, though, traditional baking skills are being lost because it's so easy to pick up mass-produced baked goods with your weekly supermarket shop. Once you've made our homemade versions, though, you'll never look back!

There's a recipe for every occasion in this 'Easy Baking' chapter. For example, we think it's high time to revive the civilized tradition of afternoon tea. You could serve *Raspberry crumble cake bars*, *Frosted carrot cake* or *Autumn apple cake*. Delicious ...

And if you take a packed lunch to work, our *Toffee apple cookies* are ideal to pop into a lunchbox. Once you've made them

they only keep for a couple of days, but they're so yummy we doubt they'll be around that long anyway.

Our *Cheat's hot cross buns* beat shop-bought ones hands down and if you leave off the traditional Easter dough cross on the top, you can serve them as fruity toasted buns at any time of the year. Kids love our *Chewy flapjacks* (they're great in lunchboxes too). Our *Butterscotch apple charlotte* can be turned into a dessert just by adding a spoonful of crème fraîche or clotted cream, and a slice of our delicious *New York lemon cheesecake* is wonderful on a warm summer's afternoon. Perfect!

Toffee apple cookies

These cookies manage to be both crisp and chewy at the same time. Just one word of warning though – they will only keep for a couple of days or the toffee gets too sticky.

- Makes 24
- Ready in 30 minutes
- Not suitable for freezing

175g soft unsalted butter
140g caster sugar
2 egg yolks
50g ground almonds
85g chewy toffees, roughly chopped
85g ready-to-eat dried apple chunks,
    roughly chopped
225g self-raising flour
2 tbsp milk

1 Turn the oven to fan 170C/conventional 190C/gas 5. Using an electric whisk, beat together the butter and sugar until pale and creamy. Stir in the egg yolks, ground almonds, toffees, dried apple and flour, and mix well.

2 Roll the dough into walnut-sized balls, place them well apart on two non-stick or lined baking sheets and flatten slightly with your hand. Brush with milk and bake for 8–12 minutes until golden. Leave on the baking tin to firm up for 5 minutes, then transfer to a wire rack and leave to cool completely.

Cheat's hot cross buns

What could be better at Easter than a toasted hot cross bun with melted butter? Here, we've used a bread mix to really speed up this recipe. Making the crosses for the top is easiest with a piping bag, but if you don't have one, use a plastic food bag – just make a tiny nick in one of the corners for an opening.

- Makes 10
- Ready in 15 minutes, plus rising
- Suitable for freezing

500g pack white bread mix
2 heaped tsp mixed spice
50g caster sugar
50g butter
50g mixed peel
85g currants
100ml milk
1 egg
3 tbsp plain flour
golden syrup, for brushing

1 Tip the bread mix into a bowl and stir in the spice and sugar. Rub in the butter with your fingertips, then stir in the peel and currants.

2 In another bowl, mix 100ml of water with the milk, then beat in the egg and pour into the dry ingredients. Mix to a very moist dough. Leave for 5 minutes, then cut into ten evenly-sized pieces and roughly shape into buns with oiled hands to prevent the mixture sticking too much. Although the mixture will be very moist, try not to use extra flour as it will toughen the dough.

3 Space the buns apart on two greased baking sheets, cover loosely with cling film, then leave in a warm room to rise, until about half as big again in size. This will take anything from 45 minutes to 1¼ hours, depending on how warm the environment is. Turn the oven to fan 200C/conventional 220C/gas 7.

4 When the buns have risen, make the crosses. Mix the flour with 2½ tbsp of water to make a paste. Pour into a piping bag or a prepared plastic food bag. Pipe crosses on each bun. Bake for 12 minutes until risen and golden. Trim any excess cross mixture and brush the buns with golden syrup while they are still warm. These are best eaten on the day they're made – after that, they're best toasted.

New York cheesecake

There are two kinds of cheesecake – either be baked, as here, or set with gelatine and chilled in the fridge. Our traditional American baked recipe gives a lovely light, fluffy filling.

- Cuts into 12
- Ready in 1¼ hours, plus 2 hours cooling and overnight chilling
- Not suitable for freezing

85g butter, melted, plus extra for greasing
10 digestive biscuits
250g caster sugar, plus 2 tbsp extra
three 300g packs full-fat soft cheese
3 tbsp plain flour
1½ tsp vanilla extract
finely grated rind of 1 lemon and 3½ tsp juice
3 large eggs, plus 1 extra yolk
284ml and 142ml cartons soured cream

1 Turn the oven to fan 160C/conventional 180C/gas 4. Line the base of a 23cm springform cake tin with baking parchment. Melt the butter in a medium pan. Crush the biscuits and stir into the butter with 1 tbsp of the extra sugar. Press into the tin and bake for 10 minutes. Allow to cool on a wire rack.

2 Turn the oven up to fan 220C/conventional 240C/gas 9. Using an electric hand whisk, beat the soft cheese for 2 minutes. With the mixer on low, gradually add 250g of the sugar, the flour and a pinch of salt. Mix well.

3 Add the vanilla extract, lemon rind and 1½ tsp of lemon juice, then whisk in the eggs and extra yolk, one at a time. Measure 200ml of soured cream into a jug and pour slowly into the mixture.

4 Brush the sides of the tin with melted butter and put on a baking sheet. Pour in the filling. Bake for 10 minutes, then reduce the oven temperature to fan 90C/conventional 110C/gas ¼ and bake for 25 minutes more. If you gently shake the tin, the filling should have a slight wobble. Turn off the oven and open the door for a cheesecake that's creamy in the centre, or leave it closed if you prefer a drier texture. Leave to cool in the oven for 2 hours. The cheesecake may get a slight crack on top as it cools.

5 Combine the remaining soured cream with the remaining sugar and lemon juice. Spread over the cheesecake, right to the edges. Cover loosely with foil and refrigerate for at least 8 hours or overnight. When you're ready to serve the cheesecake, run a round-bladed knife around the sides of the tin to loosen any stuck edges. Unlock the side, slide the cheesecake off the bottom of the tin onto a plate, then slide the baking parchment out from underneath.

Autumn apple cake

To make the cake look extra special, you can brush an apricot glaze over the top. Heat 3 tbsp of apricot jam in a small pan until it begins to bubble. Brush the warm jam over the top of the cake, then allow to cool before cutting.

- Cuts into 12
- Ready in 15 minutes, plus 50 minutes in the oven
- Suitable for freezing

175g butter, plus extra for greasing
3 eggs
350g self-raising flour
2 tsp ground cinnamon
175g light muscovado sugar
3 eating apples, 2 cored and chopped and
    1 thinly sliced
100g stoned dates, chopped
100g hazelnuts, roughly chopped

1 Turn the oven to fan 160C/conventional 180C/gas 4. Lightly butter a 20cm loose-based cake tin, then line the bottom with a buttered circle of baking parchment.

2 Melt the butter, cool for 5 minutes, beat in the eggs and set aside. In a separate bowl, thoroughly mix the flour, cinnamon and sugar, then stir in the chopped apples with the dates and half the hazelnuts. Mix well.

3 Pour the butter and eggs into the flour mixture and gently stir to combine thoroughly. Spoon into the prepared tin and smooth the top with a knife.

4 Arrange the sliced apple on top of the cake and sprinkle over the remaining hazelnuts. Bake for 50 minutes or until the cake is cooked and risen. A skewer should come out clean when inserted into the centre and the slices of apple on the top should have curled at the edges. Allow the cake to cool in the tin for 5 minutes.

Raspberry crumble cake bars

The semolina will absorb juice from the raspberries and helps stop the bars becoming soggy if you don't eat them immediately, but you can leave it out, if you like.

- Makes 24 squares
- Ready in 15 minutes, plus 50 minutes in the oven
- Suitable for freezing

435g plain flour
150g caster sugar
325g butter, diced
2 eggs, beaten
85g porridge oats
1 rounded tsp ground cinnamon
grated rind of 1 lemon
2 rounded tbsp semolina
500g fresh raspberries

1 Turn the oven to fan 180C/conventional 200C/gas 6. Butter a 23 x 33cm baking tin. Put 350g of the flour, 50g of the sugar and 200g of the butter in a food processor, and blitz until the mixture resembles breadcrumbs. Add the eggs and process until just combined. Press the dough into the tin and level out.

2 Mix the remaining flour and sugar with the oats, cinnamon and lemon rind, then rub in the remaining butter with your fingertips until crumbly.

3 Sprinkle the semolina over the dough in the tin, top with an even layer of raspberries and then with the crumble mix. Press down gently, trying to cover most of the raspberries. Bake for 20 minutes, then turn the oven down to fan 160C/conventional 180C/gas 4 and bake for another 30 minutes until the top is golden brown. Leave to cool in the tin for 30 minutes, then cut into squares and put on a wire rack until completely cold. These will keep for up to 2 days in an airtight container or freeze for up to 2 months.

Butterscotch apple charlotte

This is a delicious twist on a traditional English dessert. It used to be served cold, but our version is perfect served straight from the oven or at room temperature.

- Serves 8
- Ready in 1 hour 20 minutes
- Not suitable for freezing

200g butter
100g light muscovado sugar
200ml double cream
1.3kg cooking apples, peeled, cored and cut into thick slices
grated rind and juice of 1 lemon
1 large unsliced white loaf, preferably a day old
25g caster sugar
½ tsp ground cinnamon
1 egg
85g pecan nut halves

1 Melt 85g of the butter in a small saucepan. Stir in the muscovado sugar and cook over a low heat, stirring occasionally until the sugar has dissolved. Pour in the double cream. Increase the heat and boil for about 2 minutes, whisking until slightly thickened and glossy. Remove the butterscotch sauce from the heat and allow to cool completely.

2 Put the apples in a large pan and stir in the lemon rind and juice. Cover and cook on a very low heat for 8–10 minutes, until the apples are tender. Turn the oven to fan 170C/ conventional 190C/gas 5.

3 Melt the remaining 115g butter. Use a little to brush the base and sides of a deep 23cm springform cake tin. Remove the bread crusts and cut 14 thin slices from the loaf, brushing both sides of each with butter. Mix the caster sugar and ground cinnamon, and sprinkle over one side of each buttered piece of bread.

4 Lay two whole slices of bread (sugar-and-cinnamon side down) in the base of the tin. Cut the remaining slices in half. Use two to fill the spaces in the bread base, cutting them to fit. Set aside six half-slices of bread. Arrange the remainder, upright and overlapping against the side of the tin, with the sugar and cinnamon facing out. Don't leave any gaps.

5 Beat the egg in a bowl and stir in one-third of the butterscotch sauce. Add to the apples, then spoon the mix into the bread case. Sprinkle two-thirds of the pecans over it, then pour in half of the remaining butterscotch sauce. Cover with the reserved half-slices of bread (sugar-and-cinnamon-side up), cutting them to fit. Gently fold the tips of the bread in towards the middle of the pudding. Press down lightly to ensure the bread lies flat. Slide the cake tin onto a baking sheet and bake for 30 minutes. Scatter the remaining pecans on top and return to the oven for 5 minutes until crisp and golden.

6 Remove the charlotte from the oven and leave to stand for 10 minutes. Run a sharp knife around the edges of the tin to loosen it, then release the spring and ease away the sides of the tin. Lift the charlotte onto a serving plate and dust with icing sugar.

Serve with crème fraîche and the rest of the warm or cold butterscotch sauce

Frosted carrot cake

Cardamom seeds lose their flavour quickly, which is why they're sold still in their pods. It takes a few minutes to slip the seeds out and grind them up, and you can leave them out if you prefer – but they do add a lovely lemony flavour.

■ Cuts into 28 small slices
■ Ready in 25 minutes, plus 1¼ hours in the oven
■ Suitable for freezing (un-iced)

10 cardamom pods (optional)
175g self-raising flour
175g wholemeal self-raising flour
175g light muscovado sugar
1 tsp ground cinnamon
4 eggs
200ml sunflower oil
200g coarsely grated carrots
finely grated rind and juice of 1 orange
100g walnut pieces
1 medium banana, mashed
200g pack soft cheese
100g icing sugar
a little candied orange peel (optional)

1 Turn the oven to fan 160C/conventional 180C/gas 4. Grease a 19cm square, 7.5cm deep cake tin and line the base with greaseproof paper. Cut the cardamom pods, if using, in half and remove the seeds. Discard the pods and grind the seeds to a powder in a pestle and mortar. Put them in a large bowl and mix with the flours, sugar and cinnamon.

2 In a separate bowl, whisk the eggs and oil until smooth, then stir into the flour and add the carrots, orange rind and juice, walnuts and banana. Stir well until it resembles a thick batter.

3 Pour the mixture into the prepared tin. Bake for 1¼ hours until risen and firm. Cool for 10 minutes, then remove from the tin, peel off the lining paper and cool completely on a wire rack.

4 Whisk the soft cheese in a bowl until softened. Add the icing sugar, a spoon at a time, whisking until smooth. Spread the icing on the cake, swirling with a palette knife. Sprinkle over the peel, if using. The cake will keep for 4 days wrapped in foil in the fridge.

Chewy flapjacks

Bought flapjacks tend to be a bit hard and brittle, but this homemade version stays wonderfully gooey – perfect in a lunchbox, or with a cup of tea as a mid-afternoon treat.

- Makes 18
- Ready in 40 minutes
- Suitable for freezing

140g butter
100g light muscovado sugar
2 heaped tbsp golden syrup
350g porridge oats
1 level tsp ground cinnamon
½ tsp baking powder
2 medium-sized ripe bananas, peeled and
** mashed**

1 Turn the oven to fan 160C/conventional 180C/gas 4. Butter a 23 x 33cm deep baking tin. Melt together the butter, sugar and syrup in a large saucepan over a low heat, then stir in the oats, cinnamon, baking powder and a pinch of salt until well combined. Add the mashed bananas and stir to mix thoroughly.

2 Tip into the prepared tin and smooth the surface with the back of a spoon. Bake for 20 minutes or until the edges are just beginning to turn golden brown. It should feel quite firm to the touch.

3 Transfer the tin to a wire rack and cut the mixture into bars while still hot. Cool completely before removing. These will keep in an airtight tin for a week or freeze for up to a month.

Acknowledgements

Easy Cook magazine and BBC Books would like to thank the following people for providing photographs. While every effort has been made to trace and acknowledge all photographers, we would like to apologize should there be any errors or omissions.

Iain Bagwell p113; Steve Baxter p114; Peter Cassidy p8, p9 bottom left, p9 bottom right, p18, p21, p25, p78, p85, p93, p94, p99, p151, p175; Jean Cazals p170, p181; Ken Field p37, p134; Will Heap p9 top right, p14, p141; William Lingwood p13, p90, p126, p133, p137; Gareth Morgans p9 top left, p22, p29; David Munns p30, p45, p63, p76, p96, p107, p110, p121, p138, p144, p147, p152, p156, p182, p185; Myles New p42, p53, p129; Michael Paul p186; Craig Robertson p34, p38, p54, p58, p71, p72, p81, p89, p125, p160; Maja Smend p117; Roger Stowell p10, p17, p26, p33, p41, p46, p50, p57, p60, p64, p68, p82, p95 top left, p104, p118; Adrian Taylor p49; Simon Walton p148, p163; Philip Webb p130, p142, p159, p164, p167, p168, p177, p178; Simon Wheeler p66, p86, p95 bottom left, p95 bottom right, p100, p108, p155, p173; Jon Whitaker p95 top right, p103; Geoff Wilkinson p75; Elisabeth Zeschin p122

All the recipes in this book were created by the editorial team at *Good Food* or by regular contributors to the magazine, and adapted for *Easy Cook* magazine.